"A COMPLEX, FASCINATING AND ⌐...⌐"
—Clive Barnes, in the *New York Post*

"The richest, certainly the most resonant experience of the theatrical year." —*The Sunday Times Magazine* (of London)

"In the highest theatrical tradition . . . Characters and scenes and dialogue that crackle with wit . . . passion . . . power."
—Edith Oliver, in *The New Yorker*

"BRINGS THIS STILLBORN THEATRICAL SEASON TO STUNNING LIFE! Relentlessly gripping . . . The young, innocent Susan of 1944 climbs a bucolic hill to 'get a better view' of the . . . utopian future. In *Plenty*, David Hare asks that we, too, climb up to reclaim a 'better view'—but not before he's forced us to examine just how we choose to live in our own world of plenty right now."
—Frank Rich, in *The New York Times*

"Best Foreign Play of the year." —New York Drama Critics Circle

DAVID HARE is the author of seven full-length plays, among them *Slag*, *Knuckle*, and *Fanshen*, which have been produced in England and the United States. He has won numerous drama awards, and has worked as a director at London's Royal Court Theatre and the National Theatre. His latest play, *A Map of the World*, opened at the National in January, 1983.

Plenty

By David Hare

A PLUME BOOK

NEW AMERICAN LIBRARY

NEW YORK AND SCARBOROUGH, ONTARIO

PLUME TRADEMARK REG. U.S. PAT. OFF. AND FOREIGN COUNTRIES
REGISTERED TRADEMARK—MARCA REGISTRADA
HECHO EN HARRISONBURG, VA., U.S.A.

SIGNET, SIGNET CLASSIC, MENTOR, ONYX, PLUME,
MERIDIAN and NAL BOOKS are published by NAL PENGUIN INC.,
1633 Broadway, New York, New York 10019

Library of Congress Cataloging in Publication Data

Hare, David, 1947–
  Plenty.

  I. Title.
[PR6058.A678P54   1938]   822'.914   83-10542
ISBN 0-452-25462-0 (pbk.)

First Plume Printing, September, 1983

    4 5 6 7 8 9 10

PRINTED IN THE UNITED STATES OF AMERICA

For Kate

Plenty

Plenty was first performed in London at the Lyttelton Theatre on 7 April, 1978. The cast was as follows:

ALICE PARK	Julie Covington
SUSAN TRAHERNE	Kate Nelligan
RAYMOND BROCK	Stephen Moore
CODENAME LAZAR	Paul Freeman
A FRENCHMAN	Robert Ralph
SIR LEONARD DARWIN	Basil Henson
MICK	David Schofield
LOUISE	Gil Brailey
M WONG	Kristopher Kum
MME WONG	Me Me Lai
DORCAS FREY	Lindsay Duncan
JOHN BEGLEY	Tom Durham
SIR ANDREW CHARLESON	Frederick Treves
ANOTHER FRENCHMAN	Timothy Davies

Director: David Hare
Settings: Hayden Griffin
Costumes: Deirdre Clancy
Music: Nick Bicât

The New York Shakespeare Festival production of *Plenty*, presented by Joseph Papp, opened in New York at the Public Theater on October 21, 1982. The cast was as follows:

ALICE PARK	Ellen Parker
SUSAN TRAHERNE	Kate Nelligan
RAYMOND BROCK	Edward Herrmann
CODENAME LAZAR	Kelsey Grammar
A FRENCHMAN	Ken Meseroll
SIR LEONARD DARWIN	George Martin
MICK	Daniel Gerroll
LOUISE	Johann Carlo
*M. AUNG	Conard Yama
*MME. AUNG	Ginny Yang
DORCAS FREY	Madeleine Potter
JOHN BEGLEY	Stephen Mellor
SIR ANDREW CHARLESON	Bill Moor
ANOTHER FRENCHMAN	Dominic Chianese

Director: David Hare
Scenery: John Gunter
Costumes: Jane Greenwood
Music: Nick Bicât

This production of *Plenty* subsequently moved to Broadway, where it opened at the Plymouth Theatre on January 6, 1983. The only cast changes were:

CODENAME LAZAR	Ben Masters
JOHN BEGLEY	Jeff Allin
ANOTHER FRENCHMAN	Pierre Epstein

*Note: Name changed from Wong for New York production.

ONE

KNIGHTSBRIDGE. EASTER 1962

A wooden floor. At the back of the stage high windows give the impression of a room which has been stripped bare. Around the floor are packing cases full of fine objects. At the front lies a single mattress, on which a naked man is sleeping face downwards.

SUSAN *sits on one of the packing cases. In her middle thirties, she is thin and well-presented. She wastes no energy. She now rolls an Old Holborn and lights it.*

ALICE *comes in from the street, a blanket over her head. She carries a small tinfoil parcel. She is small-featured, slightly younger and busier than* SUSAN. *She wears jeans. She drops the blanket and shakes the rain off herself.*

ALICE: I don't know why anybody lives in this country. No wonder everyone has colds all the time. Even what they call passion, it still comes at you down a blocked nose.
    (SUSAN *smokes quietly.* ALICE *is distracted by some stray object which she tosses into a packing case. The man stirs and turns over. He is middle aged, running to fat and covered in dried blood.* SUSAN *cues* ALICE.)
SUSAN: And the food.
ALICE: Yeah. The wet. The cold. The flu. The food. The loveless English. How is he?
SUSAN: Fine.
    (ALICE *kneels down beside him.*)
ALICE: The blood is spectacular.
SUSAN: The blood is from his thumb.
    (ALICE *takes his penis between her thumb and forefinger.*)
ALICE: Turkey neck and turkey gristle, isn't that what they say?
    (*A pause.* SUSAN *smokes.*)

Are you sure he's O.K.?

SUSAN: He had a couple of Nembutal and twelve fingers of Scotch. It's nothing else, don't worry.

ALICE: And a fight.

SUSAN: A short fight.

(ALICE *takes the tinfoil parcel and opens it. Steam rises.*)

ALICE: Chinese takeaway. Want some?

SUSAN: It's six o'clock in the morning.

ALICE: Sweet and sour prawn.

SUSAN: No thanks.

ALICE: You should. You worked as hard as I did. When we started last night, I didn't think it could be done.

(ALICE *gestures round the empty room. Then eats.* SUSAN *watches, then gets up and stands behind her with a key.*)

SUSAN: It's a Yale. There's a mortise as well but I've lost the key. There's a cleaning lady next door, should you want one, her work's good but don't try talking about the blacks. You have a share in that garden in the centre of the square, you know all those trees and flowers they keep locked up. The milkman calls daily, again he's nice, but don't touch the yoghurt, it's green, we call it Venusian sperm.

(*Pause.*)

Good luck with your girls.

(SUSAN *turns to go.* ALICE *gets up.*)

ALICE: Are you sure you can't stay? I think you'd like them.

SUSAN: Unmarried mothers, I don't think I'd get on.

ALICE: I'm going to ring round at nine o'clock. If you just stayed on for a couple of hours . . .

SUSAN: You don't really want that, nobody would.

(*Pause.*)

You must tell my husband . . .

ALICE: You've given me the house, and you went on your way.

SUSAN: Tell him I left with nothing that was his. I just walked out on him. Everything to go.

(SUSAN *smiles again and goes out. There is a pause. The man stirs again at the front of the stage.* ALICE *stands still holding the sweet and sour prawn.*)

BROCK: Darling.

(BROCK *is still asleep. His eyes don't open as he turns over.* ALICE *watches very beadily. There is a long pause. Then he murmurs:*)
What's for breakfast?
ALICE: Fish.

TWO

ST BENOÎT. NOVEMBER 1943
Darkness. From the dark the sound of the wireless. From offstage, a beam of light flashes irregularly, cutting up through the night. Then back to dark.

ANNOUNCER: Ici Londres. Les voix de la liberté. Ensuite quelques messages personnels. Mon Oncle Albert a Perdu son Chien. Mon—Oncle—Albert—A—Perdu—Son—Chien.
(*A heavy thump in the darkness. Then the sound of someone running towards the noise. A small amount of light shows us the scene.* LAZAR *is trying to disentangle himself from his parachute. He has landed at the edge of the wood. At the back* SUSAN *runs on from a great distance, wrapped in a greatcoat against the cold. She has a scarf round her face so that only her eyes can be seen. She is extremely nervous and vulnerable, and her*

uncertainty makes her rude and abrupt.)

SUSAN: Eh, qu'est-ce que vous faites ici?

LAZAR: Ah rien. Laisse-moi un moment, je peux tout expliquer.

(SUSAN *takes a revolver from her pocket and moves towards him. She stoops down, feels the edge of* LAZAR's *parachute.*)

SUSAN: Donnez-moi votre sac.

(LAZAR *throws across the satchel which has been tied to his waist.* SUSAN *looks through it, then puts the gun back in her pocket.*)

And your French is not good.

(SUSAN *moves quickly away to listen for sounds in the night.* LAZAR *watches then speaks quietly to her back.* LAZAR *is a codename, he is of course English.*)

LAZAR: Where am I?

SUSAN: Please be quiet. I can't hear when you speak. (*Pause.*) There's a road. Through the wood. Gestapo patrol.

LAZAR: I see.

SUSAN: I thought I heard something.

LAZAR: Are you waiting for supplies?

SUSAN: On the hour. There's meant to be a drop. I thought it was early, that's why I flashed.

LAZAR: I'm sorry. We had to take advantage of your light. We were losing fuel. I'm afraid I'm meant to be eighty miles on. Can you . . . could you tell me where I am?

SUSAN: You've landed near a village called St. Benoît. It's close to a town called Poitiers, all right?

LAZAR: Yes. I think. I have heard of it you know.

(*Pause. She half turns but still does not look at him.*)

SUSAN: Hadn't you better take that thing off?

LAZAR: We are in the same racket, I suppose?

SUSAN: Well we're pretty well dished if we aren't.

Did you spot any movement as you came down?

LAZAR: None at all. We just picked out your light.

SUSAN: If you didn't see anything I'd like to hold on. We need the drop badly—explosives and guns.

LAZAR: Have you come out on your own?

(*A pause. He has taken off his jump-suit. Underneath he is dressed as a French peasant. Now he puts a beret on.*)

14

You'd better tell me, how does this look?

SUSAN: I'd rather not look at you. It's an element of risk which we really don't need to take. In my experience it is best, it really is best if you always obey the rules.

LAZAR: But you'd like me to hold on and help you I think?
(*Pause.*)
Listen I'm happy I might be of some use. My own undertaking is somewhat up the spout. Whatever happens I'm several days late. If I could hold on and be of any help . . . I'm sure I'd never have to look you in the face.

SUSAN: All right, if you could just . . .

LAZAR: Look the opposite . . . yes. I will. I'm delighted.
(*He does so.*)
All right?

SUSAN: If you could held on, I'm sure I could find you a bike.

LAZAR: Would you like a cigarette?

SUSAN: Thank you very much.
(*Pause.*)
Cafés are bad meeting places, much less safe than they seem. Don't go near Bourges, it's very bad for us. Don't carry anything in toothpaste tubes, it's become the first place they look. Don't laugh too much. An Englishman's laugh, it just doesn't sound the same. Are they still teaching you to broadcast from the lavatory?

LAZAR: Yes.

SUSAN: Well don't. And don't hide your receiver in the cistern, the whole dodge is badly out of date. The Gestapo have been crashing into lavatories for a full two months. Never take the valley road beyond Poitiers, I'll show you a side-road.
(*Pause.*)
And that's it really. The rest you know, or will learn.

LAZAR: How long have you been here?

SUSAN: Perhaps a year. Off and on. How's everyone at home?

LAZAR: They're fine.

SUSAN: The boss?

LAZAR: Fine. Gave me some cufflinks at the aerodrome. Told me my chances.

SUSAN: Fifty-fifty?

LAZAR: Yes.

SUSAN: He's getting out of touch.

(*Pause.*)

LAZAR: How has it been?

SUSAN: Well . . . the Germans are still here.

LAZAR: You mean we're failing?

SUSAN: Not at all. It's part of our brief. Keep them here, keep them occupied. Blow up their bridges, devastate the roads, so they have to waste their manpower chasing after us. Divert them from the front. Well that's what we've done.

LAZAR: I see.

SUSAN: But it's the worst thing about the job, the more successful you are, the longer it goes on.

LAZAR: Until we win.

SUSAN: Oh yes.

(*Pause.*)

A friend . . . a friend who was here used to say, never kill a German, always shoot him in the leg. That way he goes to hospital where he has to be looked after, where he'll use up enemy resources. But a dead soldier is forgotten and replaced.

(*Pause.*)

LAZAR: Do you have dark hair?

SUSAN: What?

LAZAR: One strand across your face. Very young. Sitting one day next to the mahogany door. At the recruitment place. And above your shoulder at the other side, *Whitaker's Almanack*.

(SUSAN *turns.*)

SUSAN: You know who I am.

(*The sound of an aeroplane.* SUSAN *moves back and begins to flash her torch up into the night.* LAZAR *crosses.*)

LAZAR: That's it over there.

16

SUSAN: Wait.

LAZAR: Isn't that it?

SUSAN: Don't move across. Just wait.

LAZAR: That's the drop.

(*The light stops. And the sound of the plane dies.* SUSAN *moves back silently and stands behind* LAZAR *looking out into the field.*)

SUSAN: It's all right, leave it. It's safer to wait a moment or two.

LAZAR: Oh my God.

SUSAN: What?

LAZAR: Out across the field. Look . . .

SUSAN: Get down.

(*They both lie down.*)

LAZAR: He's picking it up. Let's get away from here.

SUSAN: No.

LAZAR: Come on for God's sake . . .

SUSAN: No.

LAZAR: If it's the Gestapo . . .

SUSAN: Gestapo nothing, it's the bloody French.

(*From where they have been looking comes a dark figure running like mad with an enormous parcel wrapped in a parachute.* SUSAN *tries to intercept him. A furious row breaks out in heavy whispers.*)

Posez ça par terre, ce n'est pas à vous.

FRENCHMAN: Si, c'est à nous. Je ne vous connais pas.

SUSAN: Non, l'avion était anglais. C'est à nous.

FRENCHMAN: Non, c'est désigné pour la résistance.

LAZAR: Oh God.

(*He stands watching as* SUSAN *handling the* FRENCHMAN *very badly begins to lose her temper. They stand shouting in the night.*)

SUSAN: Vous savez bien que c'est nous qui devons diriger le mouvement de tous les armements. Pour les Français c'est tout à fait impossible . . .

FRENCHMAN: Va te faire foutre.

SUSAN: Si vous ne me le donnez pas . . .

FRENCHMAN: Les Anglais n'ont jamais compris la France. Il faut absolument que ce soit les Français qui déterminent notre avenir.

SUSAN: Posez ça . . .

FRENCHMAN: C'est pour la France.

(*The* FRENCHMAN *begins to go.* LAZAR *has walked quietly across to behind* SUSAN *and now takes the gun from her pocket. The* FRENCHMAN *sees it.*)

FRENCHMAN: Arr yew raven mad?

LAZAR: Please put it down.

(*Pause.*)

Please.

(*The* FRENCHMAN *lowers the package to the ground. Then stands up.*)

Please tell your friends we're sorry. We do want to help. Mais parfois ce sont les Français mêmes qui le rendent difficile.

FRENCHMAN: Nobody ask you. Nobody ask you to come. Vous n'êtes pas les bienvenus ici.

(SUSAN *about to reply but* LAZAR *holds up his hand at once.*)

LAZAR: Compris.

FRENCHMAN: Espèce de con.

(*There is a pause. Then the* FRENCHMAN *turns and walks out.* LAZAR *keeps him covered, then turns to start picking the stuff up.* SUSAN *moves well away.*)

LAZAR: Bloody Gaullists.

(*Pause.*)

I mean what do they have for brains?

SUSAN: I don't know.

LAZAR: I mean really.

SUSAN: They just expect the English to die. They sit and watch us spitting blood in the streets.

(LAZAR *looks up at* SUSAN, *catching her tone. Then moves towards her as calmly as he can.*)

LAZAR: Here's your gun.

(LAZAR *slips the gun into* SUSAN'S *pocket, but as he does she takes his hand into hers.*)

We must be off.

SUSAN: I'm sorry, I'm so frightened.

LAZAR: I must bury the silk.

18

SUSAN: I'm not an agent, I'm just a courier. I carry messages between certain circuits . . .

LAZAR: Please . . .

SUSAN: I came tonight, it's my first drop, there is literally nobody else, I can't tell you the mess in Poitiers . . .

LAZAR: Please.

SUSAN: My friend, the man I mentioned, he's been taken to Buchenwald. He was the wireless operator, please let me tell you, his name was Tony . . .

LAZAR: I can't help.

SUSAN: I have to talk . . .

LAZAR: No.

SUSAN: What's the point, what's the point of following the rules if . . .

LAZAR: You mustn't . . .

SUSAN: I don't want to die. I don't want to die like that.

(*Suddenly* SUSAN *embraces* LAZAR, *putting her head on his shoulder and crying uncontrollably. He puts his hand through her hair. Then after a long time, she turns and walks some paces away, in silence. They stand for some time.*)

LAZAR: Did you know . . . did you know sound waves never die? So every noise we make goes into the sky. And there is a place somewhere in the corner of the universe where all the babble of the world is kept.
(*Pause. Then* LAZAR *starts gathering the equipment together.*)
Come on, let's clear this lot up. We must be off. I don't know how I'm going to manage on French cigarettes. Is there somewhere I can buy bicycle clips? I was thinking about it all the way down. Oh yes and something else. A mackerel sky. What is the phrase for that?

SUSAN: Un ciel pommelé.

LAZAR: Un ciel pommelé. Marvellous. I must find a place to slip it in. Now. Where will I find this bike?
(LAZAR *has collected everything and gone out.* SUSAN *follows him.*)

SUSAN: I don't know your name.

THREE

*From the dark the sound of a small string orchestra gives way to the
voice of an* ANNOUNCER.

ANNOUNCER: Ici Bruxelles—INR. Et maintenant notre soirée
continue avec la musique de Victor Sylvester et son
orchestre. Victor Sylvester est parmi les musiciens anglais
les plus aimés à cause de ses maintes émissions à la radio
anglaise pendant la guerre.
Evening.
(*A gilt room. A fine desk. Good leather chairs. A portrait of
the King. Behind the desk* SIR LEONARD DARWIN *is working,
silver-haired, immaculate, well into his late forties. A knock
at the door and* RAYMOND BROCK *comes in. An ingenuous
figure, not yet thirty, with a small moustache and a natural
energy he finds hard to contain in the proper manner. He
refers constantly to his superior and this makes him uneasy.*)

BROCK: Sir Leonard . . .

DARWIN: Come in.

BROCK: A few moments of your time. If I could possibly . . .

DARWIN: You have my ear.

BROCK: The case of a British national who's died. It's just
been landed in my lap. A tourist named Radley's dropped
dead in his hotel. It was a coronary, seems fairly clear.
The Belgian police took the matter in hand, but naturally
the widow has come along to us. It should be quite easy,
she's taking it well.

(DARWIN *nods.* BROCK *goes to the door.*)

BROCK: Mrs Radley. The ambassador.

(SUSAN *has come in. She is simply and soberly dressed. She
looks extremely attractive.*)

DARWIN: If you'd like to sit down.

(*She sits opposite him at the desk.* BROCK *stands respectfully
at the other side of the room.*)

Please accept my condolences. The Third Secretary has told me a little of your plight. Naturally we'll help in any way we can.

BROCK: I've already taken certain practical steps. I've been to the mortuary.

SUSAN: That's very kind.

BROCK: Belgian undertakers.

DARWIN: One need not say more. Your husband had a heart attack, is that right?

SUSAN: Yes. In the foyer of our hotel.

DARWIN: Painless . . .

SUSAN: I would hope. He was packing the car. We were planning to move on this morning, we only have two weeks. We were hoping to make Innsbruck, at least if our travel allowance would last. It was our first holiday since the war.

DARWIN: Brock, a handkerchief.

SUSAN: No.

    (*Pause*)

BROCK: I was persuaded to opt for an embalming I'm afraid. It may involve you in some small extra cost.

SUSAN: Excuse me but you'll have to explain the point.

BROCK: Sorry?

SUSAN: Of the embalming I mean.

    (BROCK *looks to his superior, but decides to persist.*)

BROCK: Well particularly in the summer it avoids the possibility of the body exploding at a bad moment. I mean any moment would be bad, it goes without saying, but on the aeroplane say.

SUSAN: I see.

BROCK: You see normally you find the body's simply washed . . . I don't know how much detail you want me to provide . . .

DARWIN: I would think it better if . . .

SUSAN: No, I would like to know. Tony was a doctor, he would want me to know.

    (BROCK *pauses, then speaks with genuine interest.*)

BROCK: To be honest I was surprised at how little there is to do. There's a small bottle of spirit, colourless, and they simply give the body a wash. The only other thing is the stomach, if there's been a meal, a recent meal . . .

SUSAN: Tony had . . .

BROCK: Yes, he had breakfast I think. You insert a pipe into the corpse's stomach to let the gases out. They insert it and there's a strange sort of sigh.

(DARWIN *shifts*.)

DARWIN: If er . . .

BROCK: It leaves almost no mark. Apparently so they told me, the morgue attendants when they're bored, sometimes set light to the gas for a joke. Makes one hell of a bang.

DARWIN: Shall we all have a drink?

(DARWIN *gets up.* BROCK *tries to backtrack*.)

BROCK: But of course I'm sure it didn't happen in this particular case.

DARWIN: No. There is gin. There is tonic. Yes?

SUSAN: Thank you.

(DARWIN *mixes drinks and hands them round*.)

BROCK: I'm afraid we shall need to discuss the practical arrangements. I know the whole subject is very distressing but there is the question . . . you do want the body flown back?

SUSAN: Well I can hardly stash it in the boot of the car.

(*A pause*. DARWIN *lost*.)

DARWIN: What the Third Secretary is saying . . . not buried on foreign soil.

SUSAN: No.

BROCK: Quite. You see for the moment we take care of it, freight charges, and his majesty's government picks up the bill. But perhaps later we will have to charge it to the estate, if there is an estate, I'm sorry, I don't mean to interfere . . .

SUSAN: I'm sure there'll be enough to pay for it all. Tony made a very reasonable living.

(DARWIN *gets up*.)

DARWIN: Well I think we now understand your needs. I shall go downstairs and set the matter in train.

BROCK: Would you prefer it if I did that sir?

DARWIN: No, no. You stay and talk to Mrs Radley. I'll have a word with the travel people, make a booking on tomorrow morning's flight, if that suits?

SUSAN: Yes of course.

DARWIN: You will be going back with the body I assume?

SUSAN: Yes.

DARWIN: Are there other dependants? Children?

SUSAN: No.

(DARWIN *goes out. A pause.*)

BROCK: If . . .

SUSAN: He doesn't like you.

BROCK: Sorry.

SUSAN: The ambassador.

BROCK: Oh. Well no.

(*Pause.*)

I don't think he's over the moon about you.

SUSAN: I shouldn't have said that.

BROCK: No, it's just . . . Darwin thinks disasters are examinations in etiquette. Which fork to use in an earthquake.

SUSAN: Darwin, is that his name?

BROCK: Yes, the mission all thinks it's God's joke. God getting his own back by dashing off a modern Darwin who is in every aspect less advanced than the last. (*He smiles alone.*) I'm sorry. We sit about in the evenings and polish our jokes. Brussels is rather a debilitating town.

SUSAN: Is this a bad posting for you?

BROCK: I'd been hoping for something more positive. Fresher air. The flag still flies over a quarter of the human race and I would like to have seen it really. Whereas here . . . we're left with the problems of the war . . . (*He smiles again.*) Have you met any prison governors?

SUSAN: No.

BROCK: It's just they talk exactly like us. I was hoping for Brixton but I got the Scrubs. Just the same.

SUSAN: Does nobody like it here?

BROCK: The misery is contagious, I suppose. You spend the day driving between bombsites, watching the hungry, the homeless, the bereaved. We think there are thirty million people loose in Europe, who've had to flee across borders, have had to start again. And it is very odd to watch it all from here. (*He gestures round the room.*) Had you been married long?

SUSAN: We met during the war.

BROCK: I did notice some marks on the body.

SUSAN: Tony was a wireless operator with S.O.E. Our job was harassment behind the lines. Very successful in Holland, Denmark. Less so in France. Tony was in a circuit the Gestapo destroyed. Then scattered. Ravensbruk, Buchenwald, Saarbrucken, Dachau. Some were tortured, executed.

BROCK: What did you do?

SUSAN: I was a courier. I was never caught. (*She looks straight at* BROCK.) I wasn't his wife.

BROCK: No.

SUSAN: Had you realized that?

BROCK: I'd thought it possible.

(*Pause.*)

SUSAN: What about Darwin, did he realize?

BROCK: Lord no, it would never occur to him.

SUSAN: Motoring together it was easier to say we were man and wife. In fact I was barely even his mistress. He simply rang me a few weeks ago and asked if I'd like a holiday abroad. I was amazed. People in our organization really didn't know each other all that well. You made it your business to know as little as possible, it was a point of principle. Even now you don't know who most of your colleagues were. Perhaps you were in it. Perhaps I met you. I don't know. (*Pause.*)

Tony I knew a bit better, not much, but I was glad when he rang. Those of us who went through this kind of war, I think we do have something in common. It's a kind of impatience, we're rather intolerant, we don't suffer fools. And so we get rather restless back in England, the people who stayed behind seem childish and a little silly. I think that's why Tony needed to get away. If you haven't suffered

. . . well. And so driving through Europe with Tony I knew that at least I'd be able to act as I pleased for a while. That's all.

(*Pause.*)

It's kind of you not to have told the ambassador.

BROCK: Perhaps I will. (*He smiles.*) May I ask a question?

SUSAN: Yes.

BROCK: If you're not his wife, did he have one?

SUSAN: Yes.

BROCK: I see.

SUSAN: And three children. I had to lie about those, I couldn't claim them somehow. She lives in Crediton in Devon. She believes that Tony was travelling alone. He'd told her he needed two weeks by himself. That's what I was hoping you could do for me.

BROCK: Ah.

SUSAN: Phone her. I've written the number down. I'm afraid I did it before I came.

(SUSAN *opens her handbag and hands across a card.* BROCK *takes it.*)

BROCK: And lie?

SUSAN: Yes. I'd prefer it if you lied. But it's up to you.

(*She looks at* BROCK. *He makes a nervous half-laugh.*)

All right doesn't matter . . .

BROCK: That's not what I said.

SUSAN: Please, it doesn't matter.

(*Pause.*)

BROCK: When did you choose me?

SUSAN: What?

BROCK: For the job. You didn't choose Darwin.

SUSAN: I might have done.

(*Pause.*)

BROCK: You don't think you wear your suffering a little heavily? This smart club of people you belong to who had a very bad war . . .

SUSAN: All right.

BROCK: I mean I know it must have put you on a different level from the rest of us . . .

SUSAN: You won't shame me you know. There's no point.

(*Pause.*)

It was an innocent relationship. That doesn't mean unphysical. Unphysical isn't innocent. Unphysical in my view is repressed. It just means there was no guilt. I wasn't particularly fond of Tony, he was very slow-moving and egg-stained if you know what I mean, but we'd known some sorrow together and I came with him. And so it seemed a shocking injustice when he fell in the lobby, unjust for him of course, but also unjust for me, alone, a long way from home, and worst of all for his wife, bitterly unfair if she had to have the news from me. Unfair for life. And so I approached the embassy.

(*Pause.*)

Obviously I shouldn't even have mentioned the war. Tony used to say don't talk about it. He had a dread of being trapped in small rooms with big Jewesses, I know exactly what he meant. I should have just come here this evening and sat with my legs apart, pretended to be a scarlet woman, then at least you would have been able to place me. It makes no difference. Lie or don't lie. It's a matter of indifference.

(BROCK *gets up and moves uncertainly around the room.* SUSAN *stays where she is.*)

BROCK: Would you . . . perhaps I could ask you to dinner? Just so we could talk . . .

SUSAN: No. I refuse to tell you anything now. If I told you anything about myself you would just think I was pleading, that I was trying to get round you. So I tell you nothing. I just say look at me—don't creep round the furniture—look at me and make a judgement.

BROCK: Well . . .

(DARWIN *reappears. He picks up his drink and sits at his desk as if to clear up. There is in fact nothing to clear up, so mostly he just moves his watch round. He talks the while.*)

DARWIN: That's done. First flight tomorrow without a hitch.

(BROCK *stands as if unaware* DARWIN *has come back.*)

SUSAN: Thank you very much.

DARWIN: If there's anything else. There is a small chapel in the embassy if you'd like to use it before you go.

SUSAN: Thank you.

(BROCK *turns and walks abruptly out of the room.* SUSAN *smiles a moment.* DARWIN *puts on his watch.*)

Have you been posted here long?

DARWIN: No, not at all. Just a few months. Before that, Djakarta. We were hoping for something sunny but Brussels came along. Not that we're complaining. They've certainly got something going here.

SUSAN: Really?

DARWIN: Oh yes. New Europe. Yes yes.

(*Pause.*)

Reconstruction. Massive. Massive work of reconstruction. Jobs. Ideals. Marvellous. Marvellous time to be alive in Europe. No end of it. Roads to be built. People to be educated. Land to be tilled. Lots to get on with.

(*Pause.*)

Have another gin.

SUSAN: No thanks.

DARWIN: The diplomat's eye is the clearest in the world. Seen from Djakarta this continent looks so old, so beautiful. We don't realize what we have in our hands.

SUSAN: No.

(BROCK *reappears at the door.*)

BROCK: Your wife is asking if you're ready for dinner sir.

DARWIN: Right.

BROCK: And she wants your advice on her face.

(DARWIN *gets up.*)

I'll lock up after you sir.

DARWIN: You'll see Mrs Radley to her hotel?

BROCK: Of course.

DARWIN: Good-bye Mrs Radley. I'm sorry it hasn't been a happier day.

(DARWIN *goes out.* BROCK *closes the door. He looks at* SUSAN.)

BROCK: I've put in a call to England. There's an hour's delay.

(*Pause.*)

I've decided to lie.

27

(BROCK *and* SUSAN *stare at each other. Silence.*)
Will you be going back with the body?

SUSAN: No.

(BROCK *goes to the door and listens. Then turns back and removes the buttonhole. He looks for somewhere to put it. He finds his undrunk gin and tonic and puts it in there. Then he takes his jacket off and drops it somewhat deliberately on the floor. He takes a couple of paces towards* SUSAN.)

BROCK: Will you remind me to cancel your seat?

FOUR

PIMLICO. SEPTEMBER 1947
From the dark the sound of a string quartet. It comes to an end. Then a voice.

ANNOUNCER: This is the BBC Third Programme. Vorichef wrote *Les Ossifiés* in the year of the Paris Commune, but his struggle with Parkinson's disease during the writing of the score has hitherto made it a peculiarly difficult manuscript for musicologists to interpret. However the leader of the Bremen ensemble has recently done a magnificent work of reclamation. Vorichef died in an extreme state of senile dementia in 1878. This performance of his last work will be followed by a short talk in our series 'Musicians and Disease'. (*A bed-sitter with some wooden chairs, a bed and a canvas bed with a suitcase set beside it. A small room, well maintained but cheerless.* ALICE *sits on the floor in a chalk-striped men's suit and white tie. She smokes a hookah.* SUSAN *is on the edge of the bed drinking cocoa. She is wearing a blue striped shirt. Her revolver lies beside her.* BROCK *is laid out fast asleep across two chairs in his pinstripes. Next to him is a large pink parcel, an odd item of luxury in the dismal surroundings. By the way they talk you know it's late.*)

SUSAN: I want to move on. I do desperately want to feel I'm moving on.

ALICE: With him?

SUSAN: Well that's the problem isn't it?

(*Pause.* ALICE *smiles.*)

ALICE: You are strange.

SUSAN: Well what would you do?

ALICE: I'd trade him in.

SUSAN: Would you?

ALICE: I'd choose someone else off the street.

SUSAN: And what chance would you have tonight, within a mile, say, within a mile of here?

ALICE: Let me think. Does that take in Victoria Coach Station?

SUSAN: No.

ALICE: Then pretty slim.

SUSAN: Is that right?

(*They smile. The hookah smokes.*)

That thing is disgusting.

ALICE: I know. It was better when the dung was fresh.

SUSAN: I don't know why you bother . . .

ALICE: The writer must experience everything, every kind of degradation. Nothing is closed to him. It's really the degradation that attracted me to the job.

SUSAN: I thought you were going to work tonight . . .

ALICE. I can't write all the time. You have to live it before you can write it. What other way is there? Besides nicking it.

SUSAN: Is that done?

ALICE: Apparently. Once you start looking it seems most books are copied out of other books. Only it's called tribute. Tribute to Hemingway. Means it's nicked. Mine's going to be tribute to Scott Fitzgerald. Have you read him?

SUSAN: No.

ALICE: *Last Tycoon.* Mine's going to be like that. Not quite the same of course. Something of a bitch to make Ealing Broadway hum like Hollywood Boulevard but otherwise it's in the bag.

(BROCK *grunts.*)

He snores.

SUSAN: You should get a job . . .

ALICE: I've had a job, I know what jobs are like. Had a job in your office.

SUSAN: For three days.

ALICE: It was enough.

SUSAN: How are you going to live?

ALICE: Off you mostly. (*She smiles.*) Susan . . .

SUSAN: I want to move on. I do desperately want to feel I'm moving on.
(*Pause.*)
I work so hard I have no time to think. The office is worse. Those brown invoices go back and forth, import, export . . .

ALICE: I remember.

SUSAN: They get heavier and heavier as the day goes on, I can barely stagger across the room for the weight of a single piece of paper, by the end of the day if you dropped one on the floor, you would smash your foot. The silence is worse. Dust gathering. Water lapping beyond the wall. It seems unreal. You can't believe that because of the work you do ships pass and sail across the world. (*She stares a moment.*) Mr. Medlicott has moved into my office.

ALICE: Frightful Mr Medlicott?

SUSAN: Yes.

ALICE: The boss?

SUSAN: He has moved in. Or rather, more sinister still he has removed the frosted glass between our two offices.

ALICE: Really?

SUSAN: I came in one morning and found the partition had gone. I interpret it as the first step in a mating dance. I believe Medlicott stayed behind one night, set his ledger aside, ripped off his tweed suit and his high collar, stripped naked, took up an axe, swung it at the partition, dropped to the floor, rolled over in the broken glass till he bled, till his whole body streamed blood, then he cleared up, slipped home, came back next morning and waited to see if anything would be said. But I have said nothing. And neither has he. He puts his head down and does not lift it till lunch. I have to look across at his few strands of hair, like seaweed across his skull. And I am frightened of what the next step will be.

ALICE: I can imagine.

SUSAN: The sexual pressure is becoming intolerable.

(*They smile.*)

One day there was a condom in his turn-up. Used or unused I couldn't say. But planted without a doubt. Again, nothing said. I tried to laugh it off to myself, pretended he'd been off with some whore in Limehouse and not bothered to take his trousers off, so that after the event the condom had just absent-mindedly fallen from its place and lodged alongside all the bus tickets and the tobacco and the Smarties and the paper-clips and all the rest of it. But I know the truth. It was step two. And the dance has barely begun.

(*Pause.*)

Alice. I must get out.

ALICE: Then do. Just go. Have you never done that? I do it all the time.

SUSAN: They do need me in that place . . .

ALICE: So much the better, gives it much more point. That's always the disappointment when I leave, I always go before people even notice I've come. But you . . . you could really make a splash.

(BROCK *stirs.*)

He stirs.

SUSAN: I'd like to change everything but I don't know how.

(*She leans under her bed, pulls out a shoebox, starts to oil and clean her gun.*)

ALICE: Are you really fond of him?

SUSAN: You don't see him at his best. We had a week in Brussels which we both enjoyed. Now he comes over for the weekend whenever he can. But he tends to be rather sick on the boat.

ALICE: You should meet someone younger.

SUSAN: That's not what I mean. And I don't really like young men. You're through and out the other side in no time at all.

ALICE: I can introduce you . . .

SUSAN: I'm sure. I've only known you three weeks, but I've got the idea. Your flair for agonized young men. I think you get them in bulk from tuberculosis wards . . .

ALICE: I'm just catching up, that's all.

SUSAN: Of course . . .

ALICE: I was a late starter.

SUSAN: Oh yes, what are you, eighteen?

ALICE: I started late. Out of guilt. I had a protected childhood. Till I ran away. And very bad guilt. I was frightened to masturbate more than once a week, I thought my clitoris was like a torch battery, you know use it too much and it runs out.

(BROCK *wakes.*)

He wakes.

(*They watch as he comes round.*)

BROCK: What time is it?

ALICE: Raymond, can you give us your view? I was just comparing the efficiency of a well-known household object with . . .

SUSAN: Alice leave him alone.

ALICE: It's getting on for five.

BROCK: I feel terrible.

SUSAN: (*Kissing his head*) I'll get you something to eat. Omelette all right? It's only powder I'm afraid . . .

BROCK: Well . . .

SUSAN: Two spoons or three? And I'll sprinkle it with Milk of Magnesia . . . (*She goes out into the kitchen.*)

BROCK: It seems a bit pointless. It's only twelve hours till I'm back on the boat. (*He picks up the gun.*) Did I miss something?

ALICE: No. She's just fondling it.

BROCK: Ah.

(*He looks round.* ALICE *is watching him all the time.*)

I can't remember what . . .

ALICE: Music. On the wireless. You had us listening to some music.

BROCK: Ah that's right.

32

ALICE: Some composer who shook.

BROCK: I thought you'd have gone. Don't you have a flat?

ALICE: I did. But it had bad associations. I was disappointed in love.

BROCK: I see.

ALICE: And Susan said I could sleep here.

BROCK: (*Absently admiring her suit*) I must say I do think your clothes are very smart.

ALICE: Well I tell you he looks very good in mine. (*She nods at the parcel.*) Do you always bring her one of those?

BROCK: I certainly try to bring a gift if I can.

ALICE: You must have lots of money.

BROCK: Well, I suppose. I find it immoderately easy to acquire. I seem to have a sort of mathematical gift. The stock exchange. Money sticks to my fingers I find. I triple my income. What can I do?

ALICE: It must be very tiresome.

BROCK: Oh . . . I'm acclimatizing you know. (*Smiles.*) I think everyone's going to be rich very soon. Once we've got over the effects of the war. It's going to be coming out of everyone's ears.

ALICE: Is that what you think?

BROCK: I'm absolutely sure. (*Pause.*) I do enjoy these weekends you know. Susan leads such an interesting life. Books. Conversation. People like you. The Foreign Office can make you feel pretty isolated, also to be honest make you feel pretty small, as if you're living on sufferance, you can imagine . . .

ALICE: Yes.

BROCK: Till I met Susan. The very day I met her, she showed me you must always do what you want. If you want something you must get it. I think that's a wonderful way to live don't you?

ALICE: I do. (*Pause. She smiles.*) Shall I tell you how my book begins?

BROCK: Well . . .

ALICE: There's a woman in a rape trial. And the story is true. The book begins at the moment where she has to tell the

33

court what the accused has said to her on the night of the rape. And she finds she can't bring herself to say the words out loud. And so the judge suggests she writes them down on a piece of paper and it be handed round the court. Which she does. And it says, 'I want to have you. I must have you now.' (*She smiles again.*) So they pass it round the jury who all read it and pass it on. At the end of the second row there's a woman jurist who's fallen asleep at the boredom of the trial. So the man next to her has to nudge her awake and hand her the slip of paper. She wakes up, looks at it, then at him, smiles and puts it in her handbag. (*She laughs.*) That woman is my heroine.

BROCK: Well yes.

(SUSAN *returns, sets food on* BROCK's *knee. Then returns to cleaning her gun.* ALICE *tries to re-light her hookah.*)

SUSAN: Cheese omelette. What were you talking about?

ALICE: The rape trial.

SUSAN: Did you tell Raymond who the woman was?

BROCK: What do you mean?

SUSAN: I'm only joking dear.

(ALICE *and* SUSAN *laugh.*)

BROCK: I'm not sure it's the sort of . . .

ALICE: Oh sod this stuff.

SUSAN: I said it was dung.

ALICE: I was promised visions.

BROCK: Well . . .

ALICE: It's because I'm the only bohemian in London. People exploit me. Because there are no standards, you see. In Paris or New York, there are plenty of bohemians, so the kief is rich and sweet and plentiful but here . . . you'd be better off to lick the gum from your ration card.

SUSAN: Perhaps Raymond will be posted to Morocco, bring some back in his bag . . .

BROCK: I don't think that's really on.

SUSAN: Nobody would notice, from what you say. Nobody would notice if you smoked it yourself.

ALICE: Are they not very sharp?

SUSAN: Not according to Raymond. The ones I've met are

buffoons . . .

BROCK: Susan please . . .

SUSAN: Well it's you who calls them buffoons . . .

BROCK: It's not quite what I say.

SUSAN: It's you who tells the stories. That man Darwin . . .

BROCK: Please . . .

SUSAN: How he needs three young men from public schools to strap him into his surgical support . . .

BROCK: I told you that in confidence.

SUSAN: In gloves.

ALICE: Really?

BROCK: Darwin is not a buffoon.

SUSAN: From your own lips . . .

BROCK: He just has slight problems of adjustment to the modern age.

SUSAN: You are laughing.

BROCK: I am not laughing.

SUSAN: There is a slight smile at the corner of your mouth . . .

BROCK: There is not. There is absolutely no smile.

SUSAN: Alice, I will paraphrase, let me paraphrase Raymond's view of his boss, I don't misrepresent you dear, it is, in paraphrase, in sum, that he would not trust him to stick his prick into a bucket of lard.

(BROCK *puts his omelette to one side, uneaten.*)

Well is he a joke or is he not?

BROCK: Certainly he's a joke.

SUSAN: Thank you.

BROCK: He's a joke between us. He is not a joke to the entire world.

(*A pause.* BROCK *looks at* ALICE. *Then he gets up.*)

I think I'd better be pushing off home.

(BROCK *goes and gets his coat. Puts it on.* SUSAN *at least speaks, very quietly.*)

SUSAN: And I wish you wouldn't use those words.

BROCK: What?

SUSAN: Words like 'push off home'. You're always saying it. 'Bit of a tight corner', 'one hell of a spot'. They don't belong.

BROCK: What do you mean?

SUSAN: They are not your words.

(*Pause.*)

BROCK: Well I'm none too keen on your words either.

SUSAN: Oh yes which?

BROCK: The words you've been using this evening.

SUSAN: Such as?

BROCK: You know perfectly well.

SUSAN: Such as, come on tell me, what words have I used?

BROCK: Words like . . .

(*Pause.*)

Bucket of lard.

(*Pause.*)

SUSAN: Alice there is only the bath or the kitchen.

ALICE: I know.

(ALICE *goes out.* SUSAN *automatically picks up the omelette and starts to eat it.*)

BROCK: Are you going to let her live with you?

SUSAN: I like her. She makes me laugh.

(*Pause.*)

BROCK: I'm sorry, I was awful, I apologize. But the work I do is not entirely contemptible. Of course our people are dull, they're stuffy, they're death. But what other world do I have?

(*Pause.*)

SUSAN: I think of France more than I tell you. I was seventeen and I was thrown into the war. I often think of it.

BROCK: I'm sure.

SUSAN: The most unlikely people. People I met only for an hour or two. Astonishing kindnesses. Bravery. The fact you could meet someone for an hour or two and see the the very best of them and then move on. Can you understand?

(*Pause.* BROCK *does not move.*)

For instance there was a man in France. His codename was Lazar. I'd been there a year I suppose and one night I had to see him on his way. He just dropped out of the sky. An agent. He was lost. I was trying to be blasé, trying to be

tough, all the usual stuff—irony, hardness, cleverness, wit—
and then suddenly I began to cry. Onto the shoulder of a
man I'd never met before. But not a day goes by without
my wondering where he is.

(SUSAN *finishes her omelette and puts the plate aside.* BROCK
moves towards her.)

BROCK: Susan.

SUSAN: I think we should try a winter apart. I really do. I think
it's all a bit easy this way. These weekends. Nothing is
tested. I think a test would be good. Then we would know.
And what better test than a winter apart?

BROCK: A winter together.

(*Pause. They smile.*)

SUSAN: I would love to come to Brussels, you know that. I
would love to come if it weren't for my job. But the
shipping office is very important to me. I do find it
fulfilling. And I just couldn't let Mr Medlicott down.
(*Pause.*)
You must say what you think.

(BROCK *looks at* SUSAN *hard, then shrugs and smiles.*)
I know you've been dreading the winter crossings, high
seas . . .

BROCK: Don't patronize me, Susan.

SUSAN: Anyway, perhaps in the spring, it would be really nice to
meet . . .

BROCK: Please don't insult my intelligence. I know you better
than you think. I recognize the signs. When you talk
longingly about the war . . . some deception usually follows.

(BROCK *kisses* SUSAN.)
Good-bye.

(BROCK *goes out.* SUSAN *left standing for a few moments. Then
she picks up the plate and goes quickly to the kitchen.* ALICE
*comes out of the bathroom at once in a dressing-gown. She has
a notebook in her hand which she tosses the length of the room,
so it lands on a chair. She settles on her back in the camp bed.*
SUSAN *reappears at the door.*)

SUSAN: Did you hear that?

ALICE: Certainly. I was writing it down.

(SUSAN *looks across at her, but* ALICE *is putting pennies on her eyes.*)

My death-mask.

SUSAN: Don't.

ALICE: I dream better.

(*Pause.*)

SUSAN: Do you know what you're doing tomorrow?

ALICE: Not really. There's a new jazz band at the one-o-one. And Ken wants to take me to Eel Pie Island in his horrid little car. I say I'll go if I get to meet Alistair. I really do want to meet Alistair. Everyone says he's got hair on his shoulder-blades and apparently he can crack walnuts in his armpits.

SUSAN: Oh well, he'll never be short of friends.

ALICE: Quite.

(SUSAN *turns out one light. Dim light only. She looks at the parcel.*)

SUSAN: What should I be doing with this?

ALICE: If we can't eat it, let's throw it away.

(SUSAN *turns out the other light. Darkness. The sound of* SUSAN *getting into bed.*)

Your friend Brock says we're all going to be rich.

SUSAN: Oh really?

(*Pause.*)

ALICE: Peace and plenty.

FIVE

TEMPLE. MAY 1951

Music, a cello leading. The Embankment, beside a lamp, overlooking the river.

Night. SUSAN *stands, thickly wrapped. For the first time, she is expensively dressed. She is eating hot chestnuts.* MICK *appears at the*

back. He is from the East End. He looks twenty, smart and personable.
He speaks before she knows he's there.

MICK: Five hundred cheese-graters.

SUSAN: Oh no.

MICK: I got five hundred cheese-graters parked round the side.
Are you interested?

SUSAN: I'm afraid you're too late. We took a consignment weeks
ago.

(SUSAN *laughs.* MICK *moves down beside her.*)

MICK: Where we looking?

SUSAN: Across the river. Over there.

MICK: Where?

SUSAN: South Bank. That's where the fireworks are going to be.
And there's my barrage balloon.

MICK: Oh yeah. What does it say?

SUSAN: Don't say that, that's the worst thing you can say.

MICK: It's dark.

SUSAN: It says Bovril.

MICK: Oh Bovril.

SUSAN: Yes. It's meant to blaze out over London.

MICK: Surprised it hasn't got your name on.

SUSAN: What do you mean?

MICK: Everywhere I go.

(*Pause. They look at each other.* SUSAN *smiles and removes a*
napkin from her coat pocket, and unfolds its bundle.)

SUSAN: I managed to steal some supper from the Festival Hall.
There's a reception for its opening night. They're using your
cutlery, I'm happy to say.

MICK: I wish I could see it.

SUSAN: Yes, yes, I wish you could too. (*She smiles.*) I've actually
decided to leave the Festival now. Having worked so hard
to get the wretched thing on. I'm thinking of going into
advertising.

MICK: Ah very good.

SUSAN: I met some people on the Bovril side. It's . . . well I
doubt if it'll stretch me, but it would be a way of having
some fun. (*Pause.*) Would you like a canapé?

MICK: How's Alice?

SUSAN: She's very well.

MICK: Haven't seen her lately.

SUSAN: No.

MICK: She went mainstream you see. I stayed revivalist. Different religion. For me it all stops in 1919. (*He takes a canapé.*) So how can I help?

SUSAN: I'm looking for a father. I want to have a child.
(*Pause.*)
Look it really is much easier than it sounds. I mean marriage is not involved. Or even looking after it. You don't even have to see the pregnancy through. I mean conception will be the end of the job.
(MICK *smiles.*)

MICK: Ah.

SUSAN: You don't want to?

MICK: No, no I'm delighted, I'm lucky to be asked . . .

SUSAN: Not at all.

MICK: But it's just . . . your own people. I mean friends, you must have friends . . .

SUSAN: It's . . .

MICK: I mean . . .

SUSAN: Sorry.

MICK: No, go on, say.

SUSAN: The men I know at work, at the Festival, or even friends I've known for years, they just aren't the kind of people I would want to marry.

MICK: Ah.

SUSAN: I'm afraid I'm rather strongminded as you know, and so with them I usually feel I'm holding myself in for fear of literally blowing them out the room. They are kind, they are able, but I don't see . . . why I should have to compromise, why I should have to make some sad and decorous marriage just to have a child. I don't see why any woman should have to do that.

MICK: But you don't have to marry . . .

SUSAN: Ah well . . .

MICK: Just go off with them.

SUSAN: But that's really the problem. These same men, these kind and likeable men, they do have another side to their nature and that is they are very limited in their ideas, they are frightened of the unknown, they want a quiet life where sex is either sport or duty but absolutely nothing in between, and they simply would not agree to sleep with me if they knew it was a child I was after.

MICK: But you wouldn't have to tell them . . .

SUSAN: I did think that. But then I thought it would be dishonest. And so I had the idea of asking a person whom I barely knew.

(*Pause.*)

MICK: What about the kid?

SUSAN: What?

MICK: Doesn't sound a very good deal. Never to see his dad . . .

SUSAN: It's not . . .

MICK: I take it that is what you mean.

SUSAN: I think it's what I mean.

MICK: Well?

SUSAN: The child will manage.

MICK: How do you know?

SUSAN: Being a bastard won't always be so bad . . .

MICK: I wouldn't bet on it.

SUSAN: England can't be like this for ever.

(MICK *looks at her.*)

MICK: I would like to know . . .

SUSAN: Yes?

MICK: Why you chose me. I mean, how often have you met me?

SUSAN: Yes, but that's the whole point . . .

MICK: With Alice a few times . . .

SUSAN: And you sold me some spoons.

MICK: They were good spoons.

SUSAN: I'm not denying it.

(MICK *smiles.*)

MICK: And Alice says what? That I'm clean and obedient and don't have any cretins in the family . . .

SUSAN: It's not as calculated as that.

MICK: Not calculated? Several hundred of us, was there, all got notes . . .

SUSAN: No.

MICK: Saying come and watch the Festival fireworks, tell no one, bring no friends. All the secrecy, I thought you must at least be after nylons . . .

SUSAN: I'll buy nylons. If that's what you want.

(*They stare at each other.*)

MICK: So why me?

SUSAN: I like you.

MICK: And?

SUSAN: 'I love you'?

(*Pause.*)

I chose you because . . . I don't see you very much. I barely ever see you. We live at opposite ends of town. Different worlds.

MICK: Different class.

SUSAN: That comes into it.

(*There is a pause.* MICK *looks at her. Then moves away. Turns back. Smiles.*)

MICK: Oh dear.

SUSAN: Then laugh.

(*Pause.*)

I never met the man who I wanted to marry.

(*They smile.*)

MICK: It can't be what you want. Not deep down.

SUSAN: No.

MICK: I didn't think so.

SUSAN: Deep down I'd do the whole damn thing by myself. But there we are. You're second best.

(*They smile again.*)

MICK: Five hundred cheese graters.

SUSAN: How much?

MICK: Something over the odds. A bit over the odds. Not much.

SUSAN: Done.

(*Pause.*)

Don't worry. The Festival will pay.

(SUSAN *moves across to* MICK. *They kiss. They look at each*

*other. He smiles. Then they turn and look at the night. He is
barely audible.*)
MICK. Fireworks. If you . . .
SUSAN: What?
MICK: Stay for the fireworks.
SUSAN: If you like.
(*Pause.*)
MICK: Great sky.
SUSAN: Yes.
MICK: The light. Those dots.
SUSAN: A mackerel sky.
MICK: What?
SUSAN: That's what they call it. A mackerel sky.

SIX

PIMLICO. DECEMBER 1952
From the dark the sound of Charlie Parker and his saxophone.
    *Night. The bed-sitting room transformed. The beds have gone and
the room is much more comforting. Three people.* SUSAN *is working at
her desk which is covered with papers and drawings.* ALICE *is standing
over a table which has been cleared so that she may paint the naked
body of* LOUISE *who lies stretched across its top. She is in her late teens,
from Liverpool.* ALICE *is a good way on with the job. The record ends.*

SUSAN: This is hell.
ALICE: No doubt.
SUSAN: I am living in hell.
    (SUSAN *sits back and stares at her desk.* ALICE *goes to the record
    player.*)
ALICE: Shall we hear it again?
SUSAN: You're only allowed it once. Hear it too much and you
    get out of hand.
ALICE: It's true. (*She turns it off and returns to painting.*) I'd give

43

that up if I were you. We have to go pretty soon . . .

SUSAN: Why do I lie?

ALICE: We have to get there by midnight.

SUSAN: What do I do it for?

ALICE: It's your profession.

SUSAN: That's what's wrong. In France . . .

ALICE: Ah France.

SUSAN: I told such glittering lies. But where's the fun in lying for a living?

ALICE: What's today's?

SUSAN: Some leaking footwear. Some rotten shoe I have to advertise. What is the point? Why do I exist?

ALICE: Sold out.

SUSAN: Sold out. Is that the phrase?

(*Pause.* ALICE *paints.* SUSAN *stares.*)

ALICE: Turn over, let me do the other side.

(LOUISE *moves on to her stomach.*)

SUSAN: To produce what my masters call good copy, it is simply a question of pitching my intelligence low enough. Shutting my eyes and imagining what it's like to be very, very stupid. This is all the future holds for any of us. We will spend the next twenty years of our lives pretending to be thick. 'I'm sorry, Miss Traherne, we'd like to employ you, but unfortunately you are not stupid enough.'
(SUSAN *tears up the work she is doing and sits back glaring.* ALICE *explains to* LOUISE.)

ALICE: You're all trunk up to here, OK?

LOUISE: Yeah right.

ALICE: The trunk is all one, so you just have to keep your legs together. Then you break into leaf, just above the bust . . .

LOUISE: Do I get conkers?

ALICE: No. If you were a chestnut, you'd get conkers. But you're an oak.

LOUISE: What does an oak have?

ALICE: An oak has acorns.

LOUISE: Acorns?

ALICE: But you won't need them, I promise you. We scorn

44

gimmicks. We will win as we are.

SUSAN: (*To herself*) The last night of the year . . .

ALICE: And I will sell a great many paintings . . .

    (*Pause.* ALICE *paints.*)

    Louise is staying with Emma and Willy . . .

SUSAN: Oh yes?

LOUISE: I met them in the street, I'd just left home, come down
    the A6 . . .

SUSAN: Good for you.

LOUISE: I couldn't believe my luck.

ALICE: Willy's going as a kipper, I do know that. And Emma's a
    prostitute though how we're meant to know it's fancy dress
    I really can't think.

LOUISE: I've gathered that.

ALICE: Otherwise I expect the usual historical riff-raff. Henry
    VIII, that sort of thing. We ought to walk it with a naked oak.

LOUISE: Will that friend of yours be there?

    (*A moment.* SUSAN *looks across at* ALICE *and* LOUISE.)

ALICE: No. He'll be tucked up with his syphilitic wife.

LOUISE: Why doesn't he . . .

SUSAN: Shut up Louise.

ALICE: It's all right. Ask what you want.

    (*Pause.*)

LOUISE: How do you know she's syphilitic?

ALICE: How do you think, she passed it down the line.

LOUISE: Oh God.

ALICE: Or somebody passed it and I've decided to blame her. It
    seems right somehow. She's a very plausible incubator for a
    social disease. Back over.

    (LOUISE *turns again.*)

LOUISE: Why doesn't he leave?

ALICE: Who?

LOUISE: Your friend.

ALICE: Ah well if they ever did leave their wives, perhaps the
    whole sport would die. For all of us.

SUSAN: Roll on 1953.

    (ALICE *smiles and resumes painting.*)

ALICE: Actually the clinic say it's non-specific urethritis which I find rather insulting. I did at least expect the doctor to come out and apologize and say I'm sorry not to be more specific about your urethritis, but no, they just leave you in the air.

(*As she is talking* MICK *has appeared at the door.*)

MICK: I wonder, does anyone mind if I come in?

ALICE: Mick?

(MICK *moves into the room.*)

MICK: Would you mind if I . . .

SUSAN: How did you get this address?

ALICE: Do you two know each other?

MICK: Happy New Year.

(*Pause.*)

ALICE: Mick, may I introduce you to Louise.

LOUISE: Hello, Mick.

MICK: Hello, Louise.

ALICE: Louise is going to the Arts Ball, I'm painting her . . .

MICK: Ah.

ALICE: She's going as a tree.

SUSAN: Mick, I really don't want to talk to you.

ALICE: What's wrong?

MICK: Is she really going to walk down the street . . .

SUSAN: I thought we'd agreed. You promised me, Mick. You made a promise. Never to meet again.

(*A pause.* MICK *looks down.*)

MICK: I just thought . . . well it's New Year's Eve and well . . . one or two weeks have gone by . . .

SUSAN: Have you been watching the house? Is that how you found me? Have you been following me home? (*She stares across at him.*)

Look Mick I suggest that you leave, while you still have the chance.

(LOUISE *has swung down from the table.*)

LOUISE: Does anyone mind if I put my clothes on?

(*In the silence she picks up her clothes and goes into the kitchen.* ALICE *speaks quietly.*)

ALICE: She's not finished. She'll look good when it's done.

(*Pause.*)

SUSAN: I asked Mick to father a child, that's what we're talking about . . .

MICK: Oh Christ.

SUSAN: Well we have tried over eighteen months, that's right? And we have failed.

MICK: Right.

SUSAN: Which leaves us both feeling pretty stupid, pretty wretched I would guess, speaking for myself. And there is a point of decency at which the experiment should stop.

MICK: Susan . . .

SUSAN: We have nothing in common, never did, that was part of the idea . . .

MICK: It just feels bad . . .

SUSAN: The idea was fun, it was simple, it depended on two adults behaving like adults . . .

MICK: It feels very bad to be used.

SUSAN: I would have stopped it months ago, I would have stopped it in the second month . . .

MICK: You come out feeling dirty.

SUSAN: And how do I feel? What am I meant to feel? Crawling about in your tiny bedroom, paper-thin walls, your mother sitting downstairs . . .

MICK: Don't bring my mum into this.

SUSAN: Scrabbling about on bombsites, you think I enjoy all that?

MICK: Yeah. Very much. I think you do.

(*Pause.* ALICE *looks away.* SUSAN *moves quietly away as if to give it up.* MICK *calms down.*)

I just think . . .

SUSAN: I know what you think. You think I enjoy slumming around. Then why have I not looked for another father? Because the whole exploit has broken my heart.

(*Pause.*)

MICK: You think it's my fault . . .

SUSAN: Oh Lord is that all you're worried about?

MICK: You think it's something to do with me?

SUSAN: That was part of it, never to have to drag through this kind of idiot argument . . .

47

MICK: Well it is quite important.

SUSAN: You don't understand. You don't understand the figures in my mind.

(*Pause.*)

Mick there is gentlemen's footwear. It must be celebrated. I have to find words to convey the sensation of walking round London on two pieces of reconstituted cardboard stuck together with horseglue. And I have to find them tonight.

(SUSAN *goes to her desk, takes out fresh paper. Starts work.* LOUISE *comes from the kitchen, plainly dressed.*)

LOUISE: I'll tell the others. You may be late.

(ALICE *stoops down and picks up a couple of papiermâché green branches.*)

ALICE: There are some branches. You have to tie them round your wrists.

LOUISE: Thanks all the same. I'll just go as myself.

(LOUISE *goes out. There is a silence, as* SUSAN *works at her desk.* ALICE *sits with her hand over her eyes.* MICK *sits miserably staring. This goes on for some time until finally* SUSAN *speaks very quietly, without looking up from her desk.*)

SUSAN: Mick will you go now please?

MICK: You people are cruel.

SUSAN: Please.

MICK: You are cruel and dangerous.

SUSAN: Mick.

MICK: You fuck people up. This little tart and her string of married men, all fucked up, all fucking ruined by this tart. And you . . . and you . . .

(MICK *turns to* SUSAN. SUSAN *gets up and walks quietly from the room. A pause.* ALICE *is looking at him.*)

She is actually mad.

(SUSAN *reappears with her revolver. She fires it just over* MICK's *head. It is deafeningly loud. He falls to the ground. She fires three more times.*)

MICK: Jesus Christ.

SEVEN

From the dark, music, emphatic, triumphant.

The room we saw in Scene One. But now decorated with heavy velvet curtains, china objects and soft furniture. A diplomatic home. Both men in dinner-jackets: BROCK *smokes a cigar and drinks brandy. Opposite him is an almost permanently smiling Burmese* M. WONG, *short, dogmatic. The music stops.*

WONG: Two great nations, sir. The Americans and the English. Like the Romans and the Greeks. Americans are the Romans—power, armies, strength. The English are the Greeks—ideas, civilization, intellect. Between them they shall rule the world.

(DARWIN *appears putting his head round the door. He is also in a dinner-jacket. He appears exhausted.*)

DARWIN: Good Lord, I hope you haven't hung on for me.

BROCK: Leonard, come in, how kind of you to come.

DARWIN: Not at all.

(BROCK *ushers him in.* WONG *stands.*)

BROCK: Our little gathering. We'd scarcely dared hope . . .

DARWIN: There seemed nothing left to do.

BROCK: Leonard, you know M. Wong, of course?

WONG: Mr Darwin.

DARWIN: Rangoon . . .

BROCK: Now first secretary, Burmese embassy.

WONG: An honour. A privilege. A moment in my career. I shake your hand. (*He does so.*)

DARWIN: Good, good. Well . . .

BROCK: Let me get you a drink.

DARWIN: That would be very kind.

BROCK: I'll just tell my wife you're here.

(BROCK *goes out.* WONG *smiles at* DARWIN.)

WONG: Affairs of state?

DARWIN: Yes if you . . .

WONG: Say no more. We have eaten. We did not wait. In Burma we say if you cannot be on time do not come at all.

DARWIN: Really?

WONG: But of course the English it is different. At your command the lion makes its bed with the lamb . . .

DARWIN: Hardly.

WONG: Don't worry. All will be well. Ah Darwin of Djakarta, to have met the man, to have been alone with him. I shall dine in on this for many years . . .

DARWIN: Dine out on this.

WONG: Ah the English language, she is a demanding mistress, yes?

DARWIN: If you like.

WONG: And no one controls her so well as you sir. You beat her and the bitch obeys. (*He laughs.*) The language of the world. Good, good. I have learnt the phrase from you. Out of your mouth. Good, good. I am behind you sir.

(SUSAN *appears in a superbly cut evening dress. She is dangerously cheerful.* BROCK *follows her.*)

SUSAN: Leonard, how good of you to make an appearance.

DARWIN: I'm only sorry I've been delayed.

(SUSAN *and* DARWIN *kiss.*)

SUSAN: Brock says you're all ragged with fatigue. I hear you've been having the most frightful week . . .

DARWIN: It has been yes.

SUSAN: Well don't worry. Here at least you can relax. You've met Mr Wong?

DARWIN: Indeed.

SUSAN: You can forget everything. The words 'Suez Canal' will not be spoken.

DARWIN: That will be an enormous relief.

SUSAN: They are banned, you will not hear them.

DARWIN: Thank you my dear.

SUSAN: Nasser, nobody will mention his name.

DARWIN: Quite.

SUSAN: Nobody will say blunder or folly or fiasco. Nobody will say 'international laughing stock'. You are among friends,

Leonard. I will rustle up some food. (*She smiles at* WONG.)
Mr Wong I think the gentlemen may wish to talk.

WONG: Of course, in such company I am privileged to change
sex.

(WONG *gets up to follow* SUSAN *out.*)

SUSAN: Nobody will say 'death-rattle of the ruling class'. We
have stuck our lips together with marron glacé. I hope you
understand.

(SUSAN *and* WONG *go out. Pause.*)

BROCK: Sorry I . . .

DARWIN: It's all right.

BROCK: I did ask her to calm down.

DARWIN: I'm getting used to it.

BROCK: She's been giving me hell. She knows how closely
you've been involved . . .

DARWIN: Do you think we could leave the subject Brock?

(*Pause.*)

I'm eager for the drink.

BROCK: Of course.

DARWIN: At least she got rid of that appalling wog. I mean in
honesty Raymond what are you trying to do to me . . .

BROCK: I'm sorry sir . . .

DARWIN: This week of all weeks. He had his tongue stuck so far
up my fundament all you could see of him were the soles
of his feet.

(BROCK *takes over a tray of drinks.*)

Mental illness, is it? Your wife?

BROCK: No, no she just . . . feels very strongly. Well you
know . . .

DARWIN: But there has been mental illness?

BROCK: In the past.

DARWIN: Yes?

BROCK: Before we were married. Some years ago. She'd been
living very foolishly, a loose set in Pimlico. And a series of
jobs, pushing herself too hard. Not eating. We got engaged
when she was still quite ill, and I have tried to help her
back up.

DARWIN: That's very good.

BROCK: Well . . .

DARWIN: Second marriage of course. Often stabilizes.

BROCK: What?

DARWIN: The chap in Brussels.

(*Pause.*)

The stiff.

BROCK: Ah yes.

DARWIN: You don't have to be ashamed . . .

BROCK: No I'm not it's . . .

DARWIN: In the diplomatic service it isn't as if a mad wife is any
kind of professional disadvantage. On the contrary it almost
guarantees promotion.

BROCK: Well . . .

DARWIN: Some of the senior men, their wives are absolutely
barking. I take the word 'gouache' to be the giveaway.
When they start drifting out of rooms saying, 'I think I'll
just go and do my gouaches dear,' then you know you've
lost them for good and all.

BROCK: But Susan isn't mad.

DARWIN: No, no.

(*Pause.*)

Is there a Madame Wong?

BROCK: In the other room.

DARWIN: I knew there had to be. Somehow. And no doubt
culturally inclined. Traditional dance, she'll tell us about,
in the highlands of Burma. Or the plot of *Lohengrin*.

BROCK: Leonard . . .

DARWIN: I'm sorry. I think I've had it Brock. One more Wong
and I throw it in the can.

(*Pause.*)

Do you mind if I have a cherry?

BROCK: What?

DARWIN: The maraschinos. I'm so hungry, it's all those bloody
drugs we have to take.

BROCK: Let me . . .

DARWIN: Stay.

(*Pause.*)

We have been betrayed.

(DARWIN *reaches into the cocktail cherries with his fingers, but then just rolls them slowly in his palm.*)

We claim to be intervening as a neutral party in a dispute between Israel and Egypt. Last Monday the Israelis launched their attack. On Tuesday we issued our ultimatum saying both sides must withdraw to either side of the canal. But Raymond the Israelis, the aggressors, they were nowhere near the canal. They'd have had to advance a hundred miles to make the retreat.

BROCK: Who told you that?

DARWIN: Last week the Foreign Secretary went abroad. I was not briefed. We believe he met with the French and the Israelis, urged the Israelis to attack. I believe our ultimatum was written in France last week, hence the mistake in the wording. The Israelis had reckoned to reach the canal, but met with unexpectedly heavy resistance. I think the entire war is a fraud cooked up by the British as an excuse for seizing the canal. And we, we who have to execute this policy, even we were not told.

(*Pause.*)

BROCK: Well . . . what difference does it make?

DARWIN: My dear boy.

BROCK: I mean it . . .

DARWIN: Raymond.

BROCK: It makes no difference.

DARWIN: I was lied to.

BROCK: Yes but you were against it from the start.

DARWIN: I . . .

BROCK: Oh come on, we all were, the Foreign Office hated the operation from the very first mention so what difference does it make now . . .

DARWIN: All the difference in the world.

BROCK: None at all.

DARWIN: The government lied to me.

BROCK: If the policy was wrong, if it was wrong to begin with . . .

DARWIN: They are not in good faith.

BROCK: I see, I see, so what you're saying is, the British may do anything, doesn't matter how murderous, doesn't matter how silly, just so long as we do it in good faith.

DARWIN: Yes. I would have defended it, I wouldn't have minded how damn stupid it was. I would have defended it had it been honestly done. But this time we are cowboys and when the English are the cowboys, then in truth I fear for the future of the globe.

(*A pause.* DARWIN *walks to the curtained window and stares out.* BROCK *left sitting doesn't turn as he speaks.*)

BROCK: Eden is weak. For years he has been weak. For years people have taunted him, why aren't you strong? Like Churchill? He goes round, he begins to think I must find somebody to be strong on. He finds Nasser. Now he'll show them. He does it to impress. He does it badly. No one is impressed.

(DARWIN *turns to look at* BROCK.)

Mostly what we do is what we think people expect of us. Mostly it's wrong.

(*Pause.*)

Are you going to resign?

(*The sound of laughter as* SUSAN, MME WONG, M. WONG *and* ALICE *stream into the room.* MME WONG *is small, tidy and bright.* ALICE *is spectacularly dressed.*)

SUSAN: Mme Wong has been enthralling us with the story of the new Bergman film at the Everyman.

DARWIN: Ah.

BROCK: Ah yes.

SUSAN: Apparently it's about depression, isn't that so, Mme Wong?

MME WONG: I do feel the Norwegians are very good at that sort of thing.

SUSAN: Is anything wrong?

(SUSAN *stands and looks at* BROCK *and* DARWIN.)

Please do sit down everyone. I'm sorry I think we may have interrupted the men.

BROCK: It's all right.

SUSAN: They were probably drafting a telegram . . .

BROCK: We weren't . . .

SUSAN: That's what they do before they drop a bomb. They send their targets notice in a telegram. Bombs tonight, evacuate the area. Now what does that indicate to you, M. Wong?

BROCK: Susan, please.

SUSAN: I'll tell you what it indicates to me. Bad conscience. They don't even have the guts to make a war any more. (*Pause.*)

DARWIN: Perhaps Mme Wong will tell us the story of the film. This is something I'd be very keen to hear.

MME WONG: I feel the ladies have already . . .

ALICE: We don't mind.

SUSAN: It's all right. Go ahead. We like the bit in the mental ward.

MME WONG: Ah yes.

SUSAN: Raymond will like it. You got me at the Maudsley didn't you dear?

BROCK: Yes, yes.

SUSAN: That's where he proposed to me. A moment of weakness. Of mine, I mean.

BROCK: Please darling . . .

SUSAN: I married him because he reminded me of my father.

MME WONG: Really?

SUSAN: At that point of course I didn't realize just what a shit my father was. (*Pause.*)

ALICE: I'm sorry. She has a sort of psychiatric cabaret. (SUSAN *laughs.*)

SUSAN: That's very good. And there's something about Suez which . . .

BROCK: Will you please be quiet? (*Pause.*) The story of the film. (MME WONG *is embarrased. It takes her considerable effort to start.*)

MME WONG: There's a woman . . . who despises her husband . . . (*Pause.*)

SUSAN: Is it getting a little bit chilly in here? October nights

Those poor parachutists. I do know how they feel. Even now. Cities. Fields. Trees. Farms. Dark spaces. Lights. The parachute opens. We descend.

(*Pause.*)

Of course we were comparatively welcome, not always ecstatic, not the Gaullists of course, but by and large we did make it our business to land in countries where we were wanted. Certainly the men were. I mean, some of the relationships, I can't tell you. I remember a colleague telling me of the heat, of the smell of a particular young girl, the hot wet smell he said. Nothing since. Nothing since then. I can't see the Egyptian girls somehow . . . no. Not in Egypt now. I mean there were broken hearts when we left. I mean, there are girls today who mourn Englishmen who died in Dachau, died naked in Dachau, men with whom they had spent a single night. Well.

(*Pause. The tears are pouring down* SUSAN's *face, she can barely speak.*)

But then . . . even for myself I do like to make a point of sleeping with men I don't know. I do find once you get to know them you usually don't want to sleep with them any more . . .

(BROCK *gets up and shouts at the top of his voice across the room.*)

BROCK: Please can you stop, can you stop fucking talking for five fucking minutes on end?

SUSAN: I would stop, I would stop, I would stop fucking talking if I ever heard anyone else say anything worth fucking stopping talking for.

(*Pause. Then* DARWIN *moves.*)

DARWIN: I'm sorry. I apologize. I really must go.

(*He crosses the room.*)

M. Wong. Farewell.

WONG: We are behind you sir. There is wisdom in your expedition.

DARWIN: Thank you.

WONG: May I say sir, these gyps need whipping and you are the man to do it?

DARWIN: Thank you very much. Mme Wong.

MME WONG: We never really met.

DARWIN: No. No. We never met, that is true. But perhaps before
I go, I may nevertheless set you right on a point of fact.
Ingmar Bergman is not a bloody Norwegian, he is a bloody
Swede. (*He nods slightly.*) Good night everyone.

(DARWIN *goes out.* BROCK *gets up and goes to the door, then
turns.*)

BROCK: He's going to resign.

(*Pause.*)

SUSAN: Isn't this an exciting week? Don't you think? Isn't this
thrilling? Don't you think? Everything is up for grabs. At
last. We will see some changes. Thank the Lord.

Now, there was dinner. I made some more dinner for
Leonard. A little ham. And chicken. And some pickles and
tomato. And lettuce. And there are a couple of pheasants
in the fridge. And I can get twelve bottles of claret from
the cellar. Why not?

There is plenty.

Shall we eat again?

INTERVAL

EIGHT

From the dark the voice of a PRIEST.

PRIEST: Man that is born of woman hath but a short time to live and is full of misery. He cometh up and is cut down like a flower. He fleeth and never continueth in one stay. In the midst of life we are in death. Of whom may we seek for succour but of thee O Lord, who for our sins art justly displeased?
(*The room is dark. All the chairs, all the furniture, all the mirrors are covered in white dust-sheets. There is a strong flood of light from the hall which silhouettes the group of three as they enter, all dressed in black. First* BROCK, *then* DORCAS, *a tall heavily-built, seventeen-year-old blonde and then* ALICE *who, like the others does not remove her coat.* ALICE'S *manner has darkened and sharpened somewhat.* BROCK *goes to take the sheets off two chairs.*)

BROCK: I must say I'd forgotten just how grim it can be.

ALICE: All that mumbling.

BROCK: I know. And those bloody hymns. They really do you no good at all. (*He wraps a sheet over his arm.*) Would you like to sit down in here? I'm afraid the whole house is horribly unused.
(*The women sit.* BROCK *holds his hand out to* DORCAS.)
You and I haven't had a proper chance to meet.

ALICE: I hope you didn't mind . . .

BROCK: Not at all.

ALICE: My bringing Dorcas along.

BROCK: She swelled the numbers.

DORCAS: I had the afternoon off school.

BROCK: I'm not sure I'd have chosen a funeral . . .

DORCAS: It was fine.

BROCK: Oh good.

DORCAS: Alice told me that you were very good friends . . .

BROCK: Well we are.

DORCAS: Who she hadn't seen for a very long time and she was
sure you wouldn't mind me . . . you know . . .

BROCK: Gatecrashing?

DORCAS: Yes.

BROCK: At the grave.

DORCAS: It sounds awful.

BROCK: You were welcome as far as I was concerned.

DORCAS: The only thing was . . . I never heard his name.

BROCK: His name was Darwin.

DORCAS: Ah.

(SUSAN *stands unremarked in the doorway. She has taken her
coat off and is plainly dressed in black, with some books under
her arm. Her manner is quieter than before, and yet more
elegant.*)

SUSAN: Please nobody get up for me.

(SUSAN *moves down to the front where there are two cases filled
with books on the floor.*)

BROCK: Ah Susan . . .

SUSAN: I was just looking out some more books to take back.

BROCK: Are you all right?

SUSAN: Yes, fine.

ALICE: Susan, this is Dorcas I told you about.

SUSAN: How do you do?

DORCAS: How do you do?

(SUSAN *tucks the books away.*)

ALICE: I teach Dorcas history.

BROCK: Good Lord, how long have you done that?

ALICE: Oh . . . I've been at it some time.

DORCAS: Alice is a very good teacher you know.

BROCK: I'm sure.

ALICE: Thank you Dorcas.

DORCAS: We had a poll and Alice came top.

(*They smile at each other. Unasked,* DORCAS *gives* ALICE *a cigarette.*)

ALICE: Ta.

BROCK: Where do you teach?

ALICE: It's called the Kensington Academy.

BROCK: I see.

ALICE: It's in Shepherd's Bush.

DORCAS: It's a crammer.

ALICE: For the daughters of the rich and the congenitally stupid.
Dorcas to a T.

DORCAS: It's true.

ALICE: There's almost nothing that a teacher can do.

DORCAS: Alice says we're all the prisoners of our genes.

ALICE: When you actually try to engage their attention, you
know that all they can really hear inside their heads is the
great thump-thump of their ancestors fucking too freely
among themselves.

DORCAS: Nothing wrong with that.

ALICE: No?

DORCAS: Stupid people are happier.

ALICE: Is that what you think?

(*They smile again.* BROCK *watches.*)

BROCK: Well . . .

SUSAN: Raymond, could you manage to make us some tea?

BROCK: Certainly if there's time . . .

SUSAN: I'm sure everyone's in need of it.

(BROCK *smiles and goes out.*)

Alice rang me this morning. She said she was very keen we
should meet.

ALICE: I didn't realize you were going back so soon.

SUSAN: It's a problem I'm afraid. My husband is a diplomat,
we're posted in Iran, I haven't been to London for over
three years. Then when I heard of Leonard's death I
felt . . . I just felt very strongly I wanted to attend.

DORCAS: Alice was saying he'd lost a lot of his friends.

(SUSAN *looks across at* ALICE.)

SUSAN: Yes that's true.

DORCAS: I didn't understand what . . .

SUSAN: He spoke his mind over Suez. In public. He didn't hide his disgust. A lot of people never forgave him for that.

DORCAS: Oh I see.

(*Pause.*)

DORCAS: What's . . .

ALICE: It's a historical incident four years ago, caused a minor kind of stir at the time. It's also the name of a waterway in Egypt. Egypt is the big brown country up the top right-hand corner of Africa. Africa is a continent . . .

DORCAS: Yes thank you.

ALICE: And that's why nobody was there today.

(ALICE *looks up at* SUSAN *but she has turned away*.)

I got that panic, you know, you get at funerals. I was thinking, I really don't want to think about death . . .

SUSAN: Yes.

ALICE: Anything, count the bricks, count the trees, but don't think about death . . . (*She smiles.*) So I tried to imagine Leonard was still alive, I mean locked in his coffin but still alive. And I was laughing at how he would have dealt with the situation, I mean just exactly what the protocol would be.

SUSAN: He would know it.

ALICE: Of course. Official procedure in the case of being buried alive. How many times one may tap on the lid. How to rise from the grave without drawing unnecessary attention to yourself.

SUSAN: Poor Leonard.

ALICE: I know. But he did make me laugh.

(SUSAN *looks at her catching the old phrase. Then turns at once to* DORCAS.)

SUSAN: Alice said I might help you in some way.

DORCAS: Well yes.

SUSAN: Of course. If there's anything at all. (*She smiles.*)

DORCAS: Did she tell you what the problem was?

ALICE: There isn't any problem. You need money, that's all.

DORCAS: Alice said you'd once been a great friend of hers, part of her sort of crowd . . .

SUSAN: Are they still going then?

ALICE: They certainly are.

62

DORCAS: And that you might be sympathetic as you'd . . . well
. . . as you'd known some troubles yourself . . .

ALICE: Dorcas needs cash from an impeccable source.

(*Pause.*)

SUSAN: I see.

DORCAS: I'd pay it back.

SUSAN: Well I'm sure.

DORCAS: I mean it's only two hundred pounds. In theory I could
still get it for myself, perhaps I'll have to but Alice felt . . .

ALICE: Never mind.

DORCAS: No I think I should, I mean, I think I should say Alice
did feel as she'd introduced me to this man . . .

(*Pause.* ALICE *looks away.*)

Just because he was one of her friends . . . which I just
think is silly, I mean for God's sake I'm old enough to live
my own life . . .

SUSAN: Yes.

DORCAS: I mean I am seventeen. And I knew what I was doing.
So why the hell should Alice feel responsible?

SUSAN: I don't know.

DORCAS: Anyway the man was a doctor, one of Alice's famous
bent doctors, you know, I just wanted to get hold of some
drugs, but he wouldn't hand over unless I agreed to fool
around, so I just . . . I didn't think anything of it . . .

SUSAN: No.

DORCAS: It just seemed like part of the price. At the time. Of
course I never guessed it would be three months later and
wham the knitting needles.

SUSAN: Yes.

(*Pause.*)

DORCAS: I mean to be honest I could still go to Daddy and tell
him. Just absolutely outright tell him. Just say Daddy I'm
sorry but . . .

ALICE: Wham the knitting needles.

DORCAS: Yes.

(SUSAN *looks across at* ALICE. *The two women stare steadily at
each other as* DORCAS *talks.*)

But of course one would need a great deal of guts.

(*Pause.*)

DORCAS: I mean I can't tell you how awful I feel. I mean, coming straight from a funeral . . .

(SUSAN *suddenly gets up and walks to the door, speaking very quietly.*)

SUSAN: Well I'm sure it needn't delay us for too long . . .

DORCAS: Do you mean . . .

SUSAN: Kill a child. That's easy. No problem at all.

(SUSAN *opens the door. She has heard* BROCK *with the tea-tray outside.*)

Ah Raymond, the tea.

BROCK: I have to tell you the car has arrived.

SUSAN: Oh good.

BROCK: The driver is saying we must get away at once.

(SUSAN *has gone out into the hall.* BROCK *sets the tray down near* DORCAS *and* ALICE, *and begins to pour.*)

BROCK: It must be two years since I made my own tea. Persian labour is disgustingly cheap.

DORCAS: I thought you said they . . .

ALICE: It's another name for Iran.

DORCAS: Oh I see.

(SUSAN *has re-appeared with her handbag and now goes to the writing desk. She folds the sheet back and lowers the lid.*)

BROCK: Susan I do hope you're preparing to go.

SUSAN: I will do, I just need a minute or two . . .

BROCK: I don't think we have time to do anything but . . .

(SUSAN *walks over to him.*)

SUSAN: I do need some tea. Just to wash down my pill.

(*A pause.* BROCK *smiles.*)

BROCK: Yes of course.

(SUSAN *takes the cup from his hand. Then goes back to the desk where she gets out a cheque book and begins to write.*)

ALICE: So Raymond you must tell us about life in Iran.

BROCK: I would say we'd been very happy out there. Wouldn't you Susan?

SUSAN: Uh-huh.

BROCK: I think the peace has done us both a great deal of good. We were getting rather frenzied in our last few months here. (*He smiles.*)

ALICE: And the people?

BROCK: The people are fine. In so far as one's seen them you know. It's only occasionally that you manage to get out. But the trips are startling, no doubt about that. There you are. (BROCK *hands* ALICE *tea.*)

ALICE: Thank you.

BROCK: The sky. The desert. And of course the poverty. Living among people who have to struggle so hard. It can make you see life very differently.

SUSAN: Do I make it to cash?

ALICE: If you could.

(BROCK *hands* DORCAS *tea.*)

DORCAS: Thanks.

BROCK: I do remember Leonard, that Leonard always said, the pleasure of diplomacy is perspective, you see. Looking across distances. For instance we see England very clearly from there. And it does look just a trifle decadent. (*He smiles again and drinks his tea.*)

SUSAN: I'm lending Dorcas some money.

BROCK: Oh really, is that wise?

ALICE: She needs an operation.

BROCK: What?

ALICE: The tendons of her hands. If she's ever to play in a concert hall again.

BROCK: Do you actually play a . . .

(SUSAN *gets up from her desk.*)

SUSAN: Raymond could you take a look at that case? One of those locks is refusing to turn.

BROCK: Ah yes.

(BROCK *goes to shut the case.* ALICE *watches smiling as* SUSAN *walks across to* DORCAS *to hand her the cheque.*)

SUSAN: Here you are.

DORCAS: Thank you.

SUSAN: Don't thank us. We're rotten with cash.

(BROCK *closes the case.* SUSAN *gathers the cups on to the tray and places it by the door.*)

BROCK: If that's it then I reckon we're ready to go. I'm sorry to turn you out of the house . . .

ALICE: That's all right.

BROCK: Alice, you must come and see us . . .

ALICE: I shall.

BROCK: My tour has been extended another two years. Dorcas
I'm happy to have met. I hope your studies proceed, under
Alice's tutelage. In the meanwhile perhaps you might lend
me a hand . . . (*He gestures at the cases.*) Susan's lifeline.
Her case full of books.

(DORCAS *goes to carry out the smaller case.*)

Susan, you're ready?

SUSAN: Yes I am.

BROCK: You'll follow me down?

(SUSAN *nods but doesn't move.*)

Well . . . I shall be waiting in the car.

(BROCK *goes out with the large case.* DORCAS *follows.*)

DORCAS: Alice, we won't be long will we?

ALICE: No.

DORCAS: It's just it's biology tonight and that's my favourite.

(*Off.*) Do I put them in the boot?

BROCK: (*Off*) If you could.

(SUSAN *and* ALICE *left alone do not move. A pause.*)

SUSAN: I knew if I came over I would never return.

(*She pulls the sheet off the desk. It slinks on to the floor. Then
she moves round the room, pulling away all the sheets from the
furniture, letting them all fall. Then takes them from the
mirrors. Then she lights the standard-lamps, the table-lamps.
The room warms and brightens.* ALICE *sits perfectly still, her
legs outstretched. Then* SUSAN *turns to look at* ALICE.)

You excite me.

(BROCK *appears at the open door.*)

BROCK: Susan. Darling. Are we ready to go?

NINE

From the dark the sound of a radio interview. The INTERVIEWER *is male, serious, a little guarded.*

VOICE: You were one of the few women to be flown into France?

SUSAN: Yes.

VOICE: And one of the youngest?

SUSAN: Yes.

VOICE: Did you always have complete confidence in the organization that sent you?

SUSAN: Yes of course.

VOICE: Since the war it's frequently been alleged that Special Operations was amateurish, its recruitment methods were haphazard, some of its behaviour was rather cavalier. Did you feel that at the time?

SUSAN: Not at all.

VOICE: The suggestion is that it was careless of human life. Did you feel that any of your colleagues died needlessly?

SUSAN: I can't say.

VOICE: If you were to . . .

SUSAN: Sorry, if I could . . .

VOICE: By all means.

SUSAN: You believed in the organization. You had to. If you didn't you would die.

VOICE: But you must have had an opinion . . .

SUSAN: No. I had no opinion. I have an opinion now.

VOICE: And that is?

SUSAN: That it was one part of the war from which the British emerge with the greatest possible valour and distinction.
(*A slight pause.*)

VOICE: Do you ever get together with former colleagues and talk about the war?

SUSAN: Never. We aren't clubbable.

(The Foreign Office. A large room in Scott's Palazzo. A mighty painting above a large fireplace in an otherwise barish waiting room. It shows Britannia Colonorum Mater in pseudo-classical style. Otherwise the room is uncheering. A functional desk, some unremarkable wooden chairs, a green radiator. An air of functional disuse. Two people. SUSAN is standing at one side smartly dressed again with coat and handbag; BEGLEY stands opposite by an inner door. He is a thin young man with impeccable manners. He is twenty-two.)

BEGLEY: Mrs Brock, Sir Andrew will see you now. He only has a few minutes I'm afraid.

(At once through the inner door comes SIR ANDREW CHARLESON in a double-breasted blue suit. He is in his early fifties, dark-haired, thickening, almost indolent. He cuts less of a figure than DARWIN but he has far more edge.)

CHARLESON: Ah Mrs Brock.

SUSAN: Sir Andrew.

CHARLESON: How do you do?

(SUSAN and CHARLESON shake hands.)

CHARLESON: We have met.

SUSAN: That's right.

CHARLESON: The Queen's Garden Party. And I've heard you on the wireless only recently. Talking about the war. How extraordinary it must have been.

(Pause.)

SUSAN: This must seem a very strange request.

CHARLESON: Not in the slightest. We're delighted to see you here.

(BEGLEY takes two chairs out from the wall and places them down opposite each other.)

Perhaps I might offer you a drink.

SUSAN: If you are having one.

CHARLESON: Unfortunately not. I'm somewhat liverish.

SUSAN: I'm sorry.

CHARLESON: No, no, it's a hazard of the job. Half the diplomats I know have bad offal I'm afraid. *(He turns to BEGLEY.)* If you could leave us Begley . . .

BEGLEY: Sir.

CHARLESON: Just shuffle some papers for a while.

(BEGLEY *goes through the inner door.* CHARLESON *gestures* SUSAN *to sit.*)

You mustn't be nervous you know, Mrs Brock. I have to encounter many diplomatic wives, many even more distinguished than yourself, with very similar intent. It is much commoner than you suppose.

SUSAN: Sir Andrew, as you know I take very little part in my husband's professional life . . .

CHARLESON: Indeed.

SUSAN: Normally I spend a great deal of time on my own . . . with one or two friends . . . of my own . . . mostly I like reading, I like reading alone . . . I do think to be merely your husband's wife is demeaning for a woman of any integrity at all . . .

(CHARLESON *smiles.*)

CHARLESON: I understand.

SUSAN: But I find for the first time in my husband's career I am beginning to feel some need to intervene.

CHARLESON: I had a message, yes.

SUSAN: I hope you appreciate my loyalty . . .

CHARLESON: Oh yes.

SUSAN: Coming here at all. Brock is a man who has seen me through some very difficult times . . .

CHARLESON: I am told.

SUSAN: But this is a matter on which I need to go behind his back.

(CHARLESON *gestures reassurance.*)

My impression is that since our recall from Iran he is in some way being penalized.

(CHARLESON *makes no reaction.*)

As I understand it, you're Head of Personnel . . .

CHARLESON: I'm the Chief Clerk, yes . . .

SUSAN: I've come to ask exactly what my husband's prospects are.

(*Pause.*)

I do understand the foreign service now. I know that my husband could never ask himself. Your business is conducted in a code, which it's considered unethical to break. Signs and indications are all you are given. Your stock is rising, your stock is falling . . .

CHARLESON: Yes.

SUSAN: Brock has been allocated to a fairly lowly job, backing up the EEC negotiating team . . .

CHARLESON: He's part of the push into Europe, yes . . .

SUSAN: The foreign posts he's since been offered have not been glittering.

CHARLESON: We offered him Monrovia.

SUSAN: Monrovia. Yes. He took that to be an insult. Was he wrong?

(CHARLESON *smiles*.)

CHARLESON: Monrovia is not an insult.

SUSAN: But?

CHARLESON: Monrovia is more in the nature of a test. A test of nerve, it's true. If a man is stupid enough to accept Monrovia, then he probably deserves Monrovia. That is how we think.

SUSAN: But you . . .

CHARLESON: And Brock refused. (*He shrugs*.) Had we wanted to insult him there are far worse jobs. In this building too. In my view town-twinning is the *coup de grâce*. I'd far rather be a martyr to the tsetse fly than have to twin Rotherham with Bergen-op-Zoom.

SUSAN: You are evading me.

(*Pause.* CHARLESON *smiles again*.)

CHARLESON: I'm sorry. It's a habit as you say. (*He pauses to re-think. Then with confidence*.) Your husband has never been a flyer Mrs. Brock . . .

SUSAN: I see.

CHARLESON: Everyone is streamed, a slow stream, a fast stream . . .

SUSAN: My husband is slow?

CHARLESON: Slow-ish.

SUSAN: That means . . .

CHARLESON: What is he? First Secretary struggling towards Counsellor. At forty-one it's not remarkable you know.

SUSAN: But it's got worse.

CHARLESON: You think?

SUSAN: The last six months. He's never felt excluded from his work before.

CHARLESON: Does he feel that?

SUSAN: I think you know he does.

(*Pause.*)

CHARLESON: Well I'm sure the intention was not to punish him. We have had some trouble in placing him it's true. The rather startling decision to desert his post . . .

SUSAN: That was not his fault.

CHARLESON: We were told. We were sympathetic. Psychiatric reasons . . .

SUSAN: I was daunted at the prospect of returning to Iran.

CHARLESON: Of course. Persian psychiatry. I shudder at the thought. A heavy-handed people at the best of times. We understood. Family problems. Our sympathy goes out . . .

SUSAN: But you are blocking his advance.

(CHARLESON *thinks, then changes tack again.*)

CHARLESON: I think you should understand the basis of our talk. The basis on which I agreed to talk. You asked for information. The information is this: that Brock is making haste slowly. That is all I can say.

SUSAN: I'm very keen he should not suffer on my account.

(SUSAN'*s voice is low.* CHARLESON *looks at his hands.*)

CHARLESON: Mrs Brock, believe me I recognize your tone. Women have come in here and used it before . . .

SUSAN: I would like to see my husband advance.

CHARLESON: I also have read the stories in your file, so nothing in your manner is likely to amaze. I do know exactly the kind of person you are. When you have chosen a particular course . . . (*He pauses.*) When there is something which you very badly want . . . (*He pauses again.*) But in this matter I must tell you Mrs Brock it is more than likely you have met your match.

(*The two of them stare straight at each other.*)

We are talking of achievement at the highest level. Brock cannot expect to be cossetted through. It's not enough to be clever, everyone here is clever, everyone is gifted, everyone is diligent. These are simply the minimum skills. Far more important is an attitude of mind. Along the corridor I boast a colleague who in 1945 drafted a memorandum to the government advising them not to accept the Volkswagen works as war reparation, because the Volkswagen plainly had no commercial future. I must tell you, unlikely as it may seem, that man has risen to the very, very top. All sorts of diplomatic virtues he displays. He has forbearance. He is gracious. He is sociable. Perhaps you begin to understand . . .

SUSAN: You are saying . . .

CHARLESON: I am saying that certain qualities are valued here above a simple gift of being right or wrong. Qualities sometimes hard to define . . .

SUSAN: What you are saying is that nobody may speak, nobody may question . . .

CHARLESON: Certainly tact is valued very high.

(*Pause.* SUSAN *very low.*)

SUSAN: Sir Andrew, do you never find it in yourself to despise a profession in which nobody may speak their mind?

CHARLESON: That is the nature of the service, Mrs Brock. It is called diplomacy. And in its practice the English lead the world. (*He smiles.*) The irony is this: we had an empire to administer, there were six hundred of us in this place. Now it's to be dismantled and there are six thousand. As our power declines, the fight among us for access to that power becomes a little more urgent, a little uglier perhaps. As our influence wanes, as our empire collapses, there is little to believe in. Behaviour is all.

(*Pause.*)

This is a lesson which you both must learn.

(*A moment, then* SUSAN *picks up her handbag to go.*)

SUSAN: I must thank you for your frankness, Sir Andrew . . .

CHARLESON: Not at all.

SUSAN: I must however warn you of my plan. If Brock is not promoted in the next six days, I am intending to shoot myself.

(SUSAN *gets up from her seat.* CHARLESON *follows quickly.*)

Now thank you and I shan't stay for the drink . . .

CHARLESON: (*Calls*) Begley . . .

SUSAN: I'm due at a reception for Australia Day.

(CHARLESON *moves quickly to the inner door.* SUSAN *begins talking very fast as she moves to go.*)

CHARLESON: Begley.

SUSAN: I always like to see just how rude I can be. Not that the Australians ever notice of course. So it does become a sort of Zen sport, don't you think?

(BEGLEY *appears.*)

CHARLESON: John I wonder could you give me a hand?

BEGLEY: Sir.

(SUSAN *stops near the door, starts talking yet more rapidly.*)

SUSAN: Ah the side-kick, the placid young man, now where have I seen that character before?

CHARLESON: If we could take Mrs Brock down to the surgery . . .

SUSAN: I assure you Sir Andrew I'm perfectly all right.

CHARLESON: Perhaps alert her husband . . .

BEGLEY: If you're not feeling well . . .

SUSAN: People will be waiting at Australia House. I can't let them down. It will be packed with angry people all searching for me, saying where is she, what a let-down. I only came here to be insulted and now there's no chance . . .

(CHARLESON *looks at* BEGLEY *as if to co-ordinate a move. They advance slightly.*)

CHARLESON: I think it would be better if you . . .

(SUSAN *starts to shout.*)

SUSAN: Please. Please leave me alone.

(CHARLESON *and* BEGLEY *stop.* SUSAN *is hysterical. She waits a moment.*)

I can't . . . always manage with people.

(*Pause.*)

I think you have destroyed my husband you see.

TEN

KNIGHTSBRIDGE. EASTER 1962

From the dark the sound of some stately orchestral chords: Mahler, melodic, solemn. It is evening. The room has been restored to its former rather old-fashioned splendour. The curtains are drawn. At a mahogany table sits ALICE. *She is putting a large pile of leaflets into brown envelopes. Very little disturbs the rhythm of her work. She is dressed exactly as for Scene One.*

BROCK *is sitting at another table at the front of the stage. He has an abacus in front of him and a pile of ledgers and cheque stubs. He is dressed in cavalry twills with a check shirt open at the neck.*

The music stops. The stereo machine switches itself off.

BROCK: Well I suppose it isn't too bad. Perhaps we'll keep
    going another couple of years. A regime of mineral water
    and lightly browned toast.
    (*He smiles and stretches. Then turns to look at* ALICE. *There
    is a bottle of mineral water on the table in front of her.*)
    I assume she's still in there.
ALICE: She paces around.
    (BROCK *gets up and pours some out.*)
BROCK: I told her this morning . . . we'll have to sell the
    house. I'm sure we can cope in a smaller sort of flat.
    Especially now we don't have to entertain.
    (*He takes a sip.*)
    I can't help feeling it will be better, I'm sure. Too much
    money. I think that's what went wrong. Something about
    about it corrupts the will to live. Too many years spent
    sploshing around.
    (*He suddenly listens.*)
    What?
ALICE: Nothing. She's just moving about.
    (*He turns to* ALICE.)
BROCK: Perhaps you'd enjoy to take the evening off. I'm
    happy to do duty for an hour or two.
ALICE: I enjoy it. I get to do my work. A good long slog for
    my charity appeal. And I've rather fallen out with all those
    people I knew. And most of them go off on the
    Aldermaston March.
BROCK: Really? Of course. Easter weekend.
    (*He picks his way through the remains of an Indian takeaway
    meal which is on* ALICE'*s table, searching for good scraps.*

ALICE: Except for Alistair and I've no intention of spending an evening with him, or her as he's taken to calling himself.

BROCK: How come?

ALICE: Apparently he's just had his penis removed.

BROCK: Voluntarily? It's what he intended I mean?

ALICE: I believe. In Morocco. And replaced with a sort of pink plastic envelope, I haven't seen it, he says he keeps the shopping list in there, tucks five pound notes away so he says.

BROCK: I thought that strange young girl of yours would ring.
(ALICE *looks up for a moment from her work.*)

ALICE: No, no. She decided to move on. There's some appalling politician I'm told. On the paedophiliac wing of the Tory party. She's going to spend the summer swabbing the deck on his yacht. Pleasuring his enormous underside. It's what she always wanted. The fat. The inane.
(*She looks up again.*)
If you've nothing to do you could give a hand with these.
(BROCK *takes no notice, casts aside the scraps.*)

BROCK: Looking back, I seem to have been eating all the time. My years in the Foreign Service I mean. I don't think I missed a single canapé. Not one. The silver tray flashed and bang, I was there.

ALICE: Do you miss it?

BROCK: Almost all the time. There's not much glamour in insurance you know.
(*He smiles.*)
Something in the Foreign Office suited my style. Whatever horrible things people say. At least they were hypocrites, I do value that now. Hypocrisy does keep things pleasant for at least part of the time. Whereas down in the City they don't even try.

ALICE: You chose it.

BROCK: That's right. That isn't so strange. The strange bit is always . . . why I remain.
(*He stands staring a moment.*)
Still, it gives her something new to despise. The sad thing is this time . . . I despise it as well.

(ALICE *reaches for a typed list of names, pushes aside the pile of envelopes.*)

ALICE: Eight hundred addresses, eight hundred names . . .

(BROCK *turns and looks at her.*)

BROCK: You were never attracted? A regular job?

ALICE: I never had time. Too busy relating to various young men. Falling in and out of love, turns out to be like any other career.

(*She looks up.*)

I had an idea that lust . . . that lust was very good. And could be made simple. And cheering. And light. Perhaps I was simply out of my time.

BROCK: You speak as if it's over.

ALICE: I've no doubt it is.

(*Pause.*)

BROCK: How long since anyone took a look next door?

ALICE: That's why I think it may be time to do good.

(SUSAN *opens the door, standing dressed as for Scene One. She is a little dusty.*)

SUSAN: I need to ask you to move out of here. I am in temporary need of this room. You can go wherever you like. And pretty soon also . . . you're welcome to return.

(*She goes off at once to the desk where she picks items off the surface and throws them quietly into cubbyholes.* ALICE *is looking at* BROCK.)

BROCK: You'd better tell me, Susan, what you've done to your hands.

SUSAN: I've just been taking some paper from the wall.

BROCK: There's blood.

SUSAN: A fingernail.

(*Pause.*)

BROCK: Susan, what have you actually done?

(BROCK *gets up and goes to the door, looks down the corridor.* SUSAN *stands facing the desk, speaks quietly.*)

SUSAN: I thought as we were going to get rid of the house . . . and I couldn't stand any of the things that were there . . .

(*He turns back into the room. She turns and looks at him.*)

Now what's best to be doing in here?

(BROCK *looks at her, speaks as quietly.*)

BROCK: Could you look in the drawer please, Alice, there's some Nembutal . . .

ALICE: I'm not sure we should . . .

BROCK: I shan't ask you again.

(ALICE *slides open the drawer, puts a small bottle of pills on the table.* BROCK *moves a pace towards* SUSAN.)

Listen, if we're going to have to sell this house . . .

SUSAN: You yourself said it, I've often heard you say, it's money that did it, it's money that rots. That we've all lived like camels off the fat in our humps. Well, then, isn't the best thing to do . . . to turn round simply and give the house away?

(*She smiles.*)

Alice, would this place suit your needs? Somewhere to set down all your unmarried mothers. If we lay out mattresses, mattresses on the floor . . .

ALICE: Well, I . . .

SUSAN: Don't your women need a place to live?

(*Without warning she raises her arms above her head.*)

By our own hands.

(*Pause.*)

Of our own free will. An Iranian vase. A small wooden Buddha. Twelve marble birds copied from an Ottoman king.

(*Pause.*)

How can they be any possible use? Look out the bedroom window, I've thrown them away.

(*She opens the door and goes at once into the corridor. At once* BROCK *crosses the room to the desk to look for his address book.* ALICE *starts clearing up the leaflets and envelopes on the table in front of her.*)

BROCK: I suppose you conspired.

ALICE: Not at all.

BROCK: Well, really?

ALICE: That was the first that I've heard.

BROCK: In that case, please, you might give me some help. Find out what else she's been doing out there.

(SUSAN *reappears dragging in two packing cases, already half full. She then starts gathering objects from around the room.*)

SUSAN: Cutlery, crockery, lampshades and books, books, books. Encyclopaedias. Clutter. Meaningless. A universe of things. (*She starts to throw them one by one into the crates.*) Mosquito nets, golf clubs, photographs. China. Marble. Glass. Mementoes in stone. What is this shit? What are these godforsaken bloody awful things?

(BROCK *turns, still speaking quietly.*)

BROCK: Which is the braver? To live as I do? Or never, ever to face life like you? (*He holds up the small card he has found.*) This is the doctor's number, my dear. With my permission he can put you inside. I am quite capable of doing it tonight. So why don't you start to put all those things back? (*A pause.* SUSAN *looks at him, then to* ALICE.)

SUSAN: Alice, would your women value my clothes?

ALICE: Well, I . . .

SUSAN: It sounds fairly silly, I have thirteen evening dresses though.

BROCK: Susan.

SUSAN: Obviously not much use as they are. But possibly they could be re-cut. Re-sewn? (*She reaches out and with one hand picks up an ornament from the mantelpiece which she throws with a crash into the crate. A pause.*)

BROCK: Your life is selfish, self-interested gain. That's the most charitable interpretation to hand. You claim to be protecting some personal ideal, always at a cost of almost infinite pain to everyone around you. You are selfish, brutish, unkind. Jealous of other people's happiness as well, determined to destroy other ways of happiness they find. I've spent fifteen years of my life trying to help you, simply trying to be kind, and my great comfort has been that I am waiting for some indication from you . . . some sign that you have valued this kindness of mine. Some love perhaps. Insane. (*He smiles.*) And yet . . . I really shan't ever give up, I won't surrender

till you're well again. And that to me would mean your admitting one thing: that in the life you have led you have utterly failed, failed in the very, very heart of your life. Admit it. Then perhaps you might really move on.
(*Pause.*)
Now I'm going to go and give our doctor a ring. I plan at last to beat you at your own kind of game. I am going to play as dirtily and ruthlessly as you. And this time I am certainly not giving in.
(BROCK *goes out. A pause.*)

SUSAN: Well.
(*Pause.*)
Well, goodness. What's best to do?
(*Pause.*)
What's the best way to start stripping this room?
(SUSAN *doesn't move.* ALICE *stands watching.*)

ALICE: Susan, I think you should get out of this house.

SUSAN: Of course.

ALICE: I'll help you. Any way I can.

SUSAN: Well, that's very kind.

ALICE: If you . . .

SUSAN: I'll be going just as soon as this job is done.
(*Pause.*)

ALICE: Listen, if Raymond really means what he says . . .
(SUSAN *turns and looks straight at* ALICE.)
You haven't even asked me, Susan, you see. You haven't asked me yet what I think of the idea.
(SUSAN *frowns.*)

SUSAN: Really, Alice, I shouldn't need to ask. It's a very sad day when one can't help the poor.
(ALICE *suddenly starts to laugh.* SUSAN *sets off across the room, resuming a completely normal social manner.*)

ALICE: For God's sake, Susan, he'll put you in the bin.

SUSAN: Don't be silly, Alice, it's Easter weekend. It must have occurred to you . . . the doctor's away.
(BROCK *reappears at the open door, the address book in his hand.* SUSAN *turns to him.*)
All right, Raymond? Anything I can do? I've managed to

rout out some whisky over here.

(*She sets the bottle down on the table, next to the Nembutal.*)
Alice was just saying she might slip out for a while. Give us
a chance to sort our problems out. I'm sure if we had a
really serious talk . . . I could keep going till morning.
Couldn't you?

(SUSAN *turns to* ALICE.)
All right, Alice?

ALICE: Yes. Yes, of course. I'm going, I'm just on my way.

(*She picks up her coat and heads for the door.*)
All right if I get back in an hour or two? I don't like to feel
I'm intruding. You know?

(*She smiles at* SUSAN. *Then closes the door.* SUSAN *at once goes
back to the table.* BROCK *stands watching her.*)

SUSAN: Now, Raymond. Good. Let's look at this thing.

(SUSAN *pours out a spectacularly large scotch, filling the glass to
the very rim. Then she pushes it a few inches across the table
to* BROCK.)
Where would be the best place to begin?

ELEVEN

BLACKPOOL. JUNE 1962
From the dark music. Then silence. Two voices in the dark.

LAZAR: Susan. Susan. Feel who I am.

SUSAN: I know. I know who you are. How could you be anyone
else but Lazar?

(*And a small bedside light comes on.* LAZAR *and* SUSAN *are
lying sideways across a double bed, facing opposite ways. They
are in a sparsely furnished and decaying room.* LAZAR *is in his
coat, facing away from us as he reaches for the nightlight.*
SUSAN *is also fully dressed, in a big black man's overcoat, her
hair wild, her dress crumpled round her thighs. The bedside*

light barely illuminates them at all.)
Jesus. Jesus. To be happy again.
(*At once* SUSAN *gets up and goes into what must be the
bathroom. A shaft of yellow light from the doorway falls across
the bed.*)

LAZAR: Don't take your clothes off whatever you do.

SUSAN: (*Off*) Of course not.

LAZAR: That would spoil it hopelessly for me.

SUSAN: (*Off*) I'm getting my cigarettes. I roll my own . . .

LAZAR: Goodness me.

SUSAN: Tell you, there are no fucking flies on me.
(*She has reappeared with her holdall which is crumpled and
stained. She sits cross-legged on the end of the bed. She starts
to roll two cigarettes.*)

LAZAR: I am glad I found you.

SUSAN: I'm just glad I came.

LAZAR: This place is filthy.

SUSAN: It's a cheap hotel.

LAZAR: They seem to serve you dust on almost everything.

SUSAN: You should be grateful for dust, did you know? If it
weren't for all the dust in the atmosphere, human beings
would be killed by the heat of the sun.

LAZAR: In Blackpool?

SUSAN: Well . . .

LAZAR: Are you kidding me?
(SUSAN *reaches into the overcoat pocket.*)

SUSAN: I was given some grass, shall I roll it in?

LAZAR: Just the simple cigarette for me.
(SUSAN *nods.*)
I hope you didn't mind my choosing Blackpool at all. It's
just that I work near . . .

SUSAN: Don't tell me any more.

LAZAR: Susan . . .
(*Pause.*)
Will you . . . . . can you touch me again?
(SUSAN *facing away doesn't move, just smiles. A pause.*)
Do you know how I found you? Through the BBC. I just
caught that programme a few months ago. They told me

you were married and based in London now. They gave me
an address . . .

SUSAN: I left it weeks ago.

LAZAR: I know. I gather you've been out on the road. But . . . I
went, I went round and saw the man . . .

SUSAN: And how was he?

LAZAR: He looked like a man who'd spent his life with you.

SUSAN: How can you say that?

LAZAR: (*Smiles*) Oh I'm guessing that's all.
(SUSAN *smiles again*.)
He said he'd only just managed to re-claim.

SUSAN: Oh really? That's my fault. I gave the house away.

LAZAR: He said he'd had to fight to get back into his home.
There'd been some kind of trouble. Police, violence it
seems . . .

SUSAN: Was he angry?

LAZAR: Angry? No. He just seemed very sorry not to be with
you.
(*Pause.* SUSAN *stops rolling the cigarette*.)

SUSAN: Listen, I have to tell you I've not always been well. I
have a weakness. I like to lose control. I've been letting it
happen, well, a number of times . . .

LAZAR: Is it . . .

SUSAN: I did shoot someone about ten years ago.

LAZAR: Did you hurt him?

SUSAN: Fortunately no. At least that's what we kept telling him
you know. Raymond went and gave him money in notes.
He slapped them like hot poultices all over his wounds. I
think it did finally convince him on the whole. It was after
Raymond's kindness I felt I had to get engaged . . .

LAZAR: Why do people . . .

SUSAN: Marry? I don't know. Are you . . .
(*Pause.*)

LAZAR: What? Ask me anything at all.

SUSAN: No. It's nothing. I don't want to know. (*She smiles again*.)

LAZAR: Do you ever see him?

SUSAN: Good gracious no. I've stripped away everything,
everything I've known. There's only one kind of dignity,

that's in living alone. The clothes you stand up in, the world you can see . . .

LAZAR: Oh Susan . . .

SUSAN: Don't.

(*Pause.* SUSAN *is suddenly still.*)

I have to believe that there's someone, you see. Somebody else who's been living like me.

(*Pause.* SUSAN *does not turn round.* LAZAR *suddenly gets up, and goes to get his coat and gloves from his suitcase.* SUSAN *looks down at the unmade cigarette in her hands. Then she starts to make the roll-up again.*)

SUSAN: How long till dawn? Do you think we should go? If we wait till morning we'll have to pay the bill. I can't believe that can be the right thing to do.

(*She smiles.*)

Is there an early train do you know? Though just where I'm going I'm not really sure. There aren't many people who'll have me you know . . .

(*Pause.*)

I hope you'll forgive me. The grass has gone in.

(*She licks along the edge of the joint, then lights it.* LAZAR *stands still, his suitcase beside him.*)

LAZAR: I don't what I'd expected.

SUSAN: Mmm?

LAZAR: What I'd hoped for, at the time I returned. Some sort of edge to the life that I lead. Some sort of feeling their death was worthwhile.

(*Pause.*)

Some day I must tell you. I don't feel I've done well. I gave in. Always. All along the line. Suburb. Wife. Hell. I work in a corporate bureaucracy as well . . .

(SUSAN *has begun to giggle*)

SUSAN: Lazar, I'm sorry, I'm just about to go.

LAZAR: What?

SUSAN: I've eaten nothing. So I just go . . .

(*She waves vaguely with her hand. Then smiles. A pause.*)

LAZAR: I hate, I hate this life that we lead . . .

SUSAN: Oh God here I go.

(*Pause.*)

Kiss me. Kiss me now as I go.

(LAZAR *moves towards* SUSAN *and tries to take her in his arms.*
But as he tries to kiss her, she falls back on to the bed,
flopping down where she stays.

LAZAR *removes the roach from her hand. Puts it out. Goes over*
and closes his case. Then picks it up. Goes to the bathroom and
turns the light off. Now only the nightlight is on.

LAZAR *goes to the door.*)

LAZAR: A fine undercover agent will move so that nobody can
ever tell he was there.

(LAZAR *turns the nightlight off. Darkness.*)

SUSAN: Tell me your name.

(*Pause.*)

LAZAR: Codename.

(*Pause.*)

Codename.

(*Pause.*)

Codename Lazar.

(LAZAR *opens the door of the room. At once music plays. Where*
you would expect a corridor you see the fields of France
shining brilliantly in a fierce green square. The room scatters.)

TWELVE

*The darkened areas of the room disappear and we see a French hillside
in high summer. The stage picture forms piece by piece. Green, yellow,
brown. Trees. The fields stretch away. A high sun. A brilliant August
day.* ANOTHER FRENCHMAN *stands looking down into the valley. He
carries a spade, is in wellingtons and corduroys. He is about forty,
fattish with an unnaturally gloomy air.*

Then SUSAN *appears climbing the hill. She is nineteen. She is dressed
like a young French girl, her pullover over her shoulder. She looks
radiantly well.*

FRENCHMAN: Bonjour ma'moiselle.
SUSAN: Bonjour.
FRENCHMAN: Vous regardez le village?
SUSAN: Oui, je suis montée la colline pour mieux voir. C'est
    merveilleux.
FRENCHMAN: Oui. Indeed the day is fine.
    (*Pause.* SUSAN *looks across at the* FRENCHMAN.)
FRENCHMAN: We understand. We know. The war is over now.
SUSAN: 'I climbed the hill to get a better view.' (*She smiles.*)
    I've only spoken French for months on end.
FRENCHMAN: You are English?
    (SUSAN *nods.*)
    Tower Bridge.
SUSAN: Just so.
    (*The* FRENCHMAN *smiles and walks over to join* SUSAN.
    Together they look away down the hill.)
FRENCHMAN: You join the party in the village?
SUSAN: Soon. I'm hoping, yes, I'm very keen to go.
FRENCHMAN: Myself I work. A farmer. Like any other day. The
    Frenchman works or starves. He is the piss. The shit. The
    lowest of the low.
    (SUSAN *moves forward a little, staring down the hill.*)
SUSAN: Look. They're lighting fires in the square. And children . . .

coming out with burning sticks.

(*Pause.*)

Have you seen anything as beautiful as this?

(SUSAN *stands looking out. The* FRENCHMAN *mumbles ill-humouredly.*)

FRENCHMAN: The harvest is not good again this year.

SUSAN: I'm sorry.

(*The* FRENCHMAN *shrugs.*)

FRENCHMAN: As I expect. The land is very poor. I have to work each moment of the day.

SUSAN: But you'll be glad I think. You're glad as well?

(SUSAN *turns, so the* FRENCHMAN *cannot avoid the question. He reluctantly concedes.*)

FRENCHMAN: I'm glad. Is something good, is true. (*He looks puzzled.*) The English . . . have no feelings, yes? Are stiff.

SUSAN: They hide them, hide them from the world.

FRENCHMAN: Is stupid.

SUSAN: Stupid, yes. It may be . . .

(*Pause.*)

FRENCHMAN: Huh?

SUSAN: That things will quickly change. We have grown up. We will improve our world.

(*The* FRENCHMAN *stares at* SUSAN. *Then offers gravely:*)

FRENCHMAN: Perhaps . . . perhaps you like some soup. My wife.

SUSAN: All right.

(SUSAN *smiles. They look at each other, about to go.*)

FRENCHMAN: The walk is down the hill.

SUSAN: My friend.

(*Pause.*)

There will be days and days and days like this.

A NOTE ON PERFORMANCE

This is a note for those of you who are planning to stage *Plenty*, to explain my own experience of what its peculiar problems are.

It's a common criticism of my work that I write about women whom I find admirable, but whom the audience dislikes. The truth is more complicated than that, but it is true that large sections of an English audience, particularly the men, are predisposed to find Susan Traherne unsympathetic, and it is also true that it is possible to play the part rather stridently, even forbiddingly, so that the audience watches and is not engaged. This was never my intention.

I planned a play in twelve scenes, in which there would be twelve dramatic actions. Each of these actions is intended to be ambiguous, and it is up to the audience to decide what they feel about each event. For example, in Scene Three, there will be some who feel that Susan does the kindest possible thing in sparing her lover's wife the knowledge of the circumstances of his death; but others may feel that the manner in which she disposes of the corpse is a little heartless. Again, in Scene Four you may feel that the way she gets rid of her boyfriend is stylish, and almost exemplary in its lack of hurtfulness; or you may feel it is crude and dishonest. This ambiguity is central to the idea of the play. The audience is asked to make its own mind up about each of the actions. In the act of judging the audience learns something about its own values.

It is therefore important that a balance of sympathy is maintained throughout the evening, and that the actress playing Susan puts the case for her as strongly as she can. The case against her makes itself, or is made by the other characters. This deliberate policy of pulling the audience one way and then another will work as long as the director has thought out exactly what the action is in each scene, and tried to present it as clearly as possible. For example, the action crystallizes in Scene Three at the moment when Susan hands over the card; in Scene Four when she lies bare-faced to Brock about letting Mr Medlicott down.

The time-scheme of the play is not as intimidating to audiences as it at first appears. Clues are built into each scene to tell you where you are, and how many years have passed. If the actors show the changes in their characters clearly enough, the audience will accept the passage of time quite easily. Brock and Alice both travel a great distance in the play. Alice is intended to be a historically accurate character, a bohemian of the late forties, part of whose charm must in retrospect seem to be her innocence. The path of dissent which she takes is very different from Susan's because it is mostly sexual. By the end of the play she is mellow, but stranded. Brock, on the other hand, has sold out, but, crucially, is intelligent enough to know that he has. It is always a mistake to play Brock as a fool. As a young man he has a delightful ingenuousness. Only an excessive enthusiasm can explain his speeches about the mortuary in Scene Three. But the institution of the Foreign Office takes him over, and life with Susan wears him down.

The transitions from scene to scene should be as quick as possible. If the director has to choose between amplifying the design or hastening it, he should always opt for speed. To those of you who perform the play abroad, I can only say that its Englishness is of the essence. To me, when an actor asks why he does something, it is a perfectly good answer to say 'Because you are English'. Irony is central to English humour, and as a people we are cruel to each other, but always quietly.